SPRINGFIELD
MEMORIES

Published by Pediment Publishing, a division of The Pediment Group, Inc. www.pediment.com Printed in Canada

Foreword

The word "Sangamon" often has been depicted as the American Indian word for "land of milk and honey." Sangamon County's Springfield area proved to be that for the early settlers, who found rich soil, plentiful game and sufficient water and timber sources. It proved to be that again for immigrants who came from all corners of Europe to harvest the coal found so plentifully underground, as well as for those in business and service industries who came to support the growing community.

In addition, the existence of the state capital drew another pool of talent to the community in the form of legislators, lawyers, journalists and others who kept our state government working — including a man named Abraham Lincoln.

People came together from diverse backgrounds to form the greater Springfield community. From small shops to large factories, the community grew in response to the needs of its people and the world around them. While it hasn't always been easy, the pride on the faces of those pictured within this volume is evident — pride for who they became and what they accomplished.

We are grateful to the Sangamon Valley Collection at Lincoln Library for sharing its collection of photographs, to the community for sharing cherished photos and to The State Journal-Register for initiating this project of collecting images from all aspects of the Springfield community. The book certainly represents a treasury of memories of the city's development.

Nancy L. Chapin
President
Sangamon County Historical Society

Table of Contents

Street Scenes

Downtown was the heart of Springfield in the mid-19th and early 20th centuries, but it was a dramatically changed downtown over those 80 years.

Abraham Lincoln still lived in Springfield in 1859, when four three-story brick buildings dominated Sixth Street across from what is now the Old State Capitol (p.8). Bare sidewalks allowed residents to avoid the dirt streets (during the spring and fall, Springfield's mud was fabled, as were the loose pigs that frolicked in it), and "traffic" might amount to a single horse-drawn wagon.

Even before the turn of the century, though, trolley lines were snaking over paved streets, and commercial buildings were starting to climb to stratospheric heights — as much as eight stories, not to mention the 361-foot-high Statehouse.

Springfield even took advantage of the close of Chicago's Columbian Exposition in 1893 to get a good deal on four striking steel arches, which were re-erected on all four corners of the courthouse square. Aside from giving downtown a distinctive look year-round, the arches could be festooned with lights, flags and bunting for special occasions, and when carnivals stopped in town, they were a ready-made stage for trapeze artists and high-wire acts. But after a workman was electrocuted while doing repairs, the arches were taken down in 1921 and sold to a scrap-iron dealer.

By 1926 (left), Model Ts, power lines and trolley tracks filled downtown streets, vying for space with the bustle of snappy-dressed pedestrians with places to go. In just one block, you could eat lunch, buy "novelty shoes," shop for a Victrola, get your teeth fixed (by a dentist who promised to use gas) and have your choice of two different cigar stores. But if you tried to turn left onto Monroe Street, you'd better be prepared for a tongue-lashing from that traffic cop.

The people standing next to that dusty street in 1859 certainly would have been amazed by the airplane that bore a photographer aloft above Springfield in 1937 (p. 14). But they probably would have been equally astounded by the scale, breadth and vigor of the city that stretched below.

LEFT: View looking north on Fifth Street from Monroe Street, circa 1926. *Courtesy Sangamon Valley Collection, Lincoln Library*

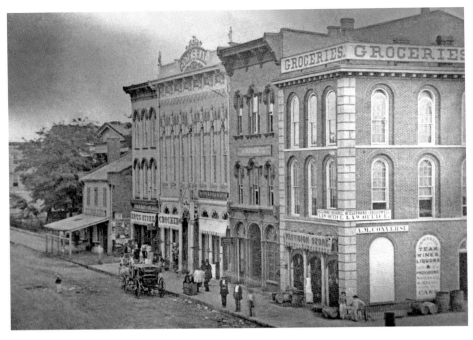

ABOVE: A view of Fifth and Monroe streets and the famous Dodds Corner, circa 1896.
Courtesy Sangamon Valley Collection, Lincoln Library

BELOW: A view of Fifth Street looking north from Adams, circa 1907. *Courtesy Jane Barry*

ABOVE: A view of Sixth Street and the east side of the public square in 1859.
Courtesy Sangamon Valley Collection, Lincoln Library

OPPOSITE: View from the Capitol dome looking east, 1903. The dome from the old courthouse is visible in the upper left corner. At the right is Capitol Avenue lined with trees.
Courtesy Sangamon Valley Collection, Lincoln Library

BELOW: Monroe Street in 1889. This view is looking west from Sixth Street.
Courtesy Sangamon Valley Collection, Lincoln Library

ABOVE: View of Fourth Street facing north from Monroe Street, circa 1918.
Courtesy Sangamon Valley Collection, Lincoln Library

TOP RIGHT: Downtown Springfield looking north on Fifth Street with arch, circa 1920. *Courtesy Don Edwards*

BOTTOM RIGHT: View looking north on Fifth Street, circa 1909. *Courtesy Sangamon Valley Collection, Lincoln Library*

ABOVE: View of Jefferson Street looking west from Fifth Street, 1920s. *Courtesy Sangamon Valley Collection, Lincoln Library*

TOP LEFT: View of Fifth Street, north of Jefferson Street, 1921. *Courtesy Sangamon Valley Collection, Lincoln Library*

BOTTOM LEFT: View of Washington Street and the north side of the public square, circa 1920. *Courtesy Sangamon Valley Collection, Lincoln Library*

ABOVE: A busy intersection in Springfield, 1926. This is Fifth and Monroe streets. *Courtesy Marlene Seaborn*

TOP RIGHT: A view of Monroe Street, looking east from Fifth Street, circa 1926. Streetcars ran on Monroe Street from 1892 through December 31, 1937. *Courtesy Sangamon Valley Collection, Lincoln Library*

RIGHT: View looking toward the Capitol from Capitol Avenue, circa 1931. *Courtesy Springfield YMCA*

FAR RIGHT: View looking south from Fifth and Jefferson streets, 1920s. *Courtesy Sangamon Valley Collection, Lincoln Library*

ABOVE: View of Fifth Street looking north in 1934.
Courtesy Sangamon Valley Collection, Lincoln Library

BELOW: View of South Sixth Street looking north from Monroe Street, circa 1934. Denton's Drug Store is on the corner of Sixth and Monroe streets. *Courtesy Sangamon Valley Collection, Lincoln Library*

ABOVE: View of the southwest corner of Fourth and Monroe streets facing southwest. This building was likely the one that housed the Conkling & Co. Illinois Hominy Mills, December 1932.
Courtesy Sangamon Valley Collection, Lincoln Library

BELOW: Bird's-eye view of Sangamo Electric Company, 1920s. This photo was taken before Lanphier High School was built in the late 1930s. The view looks northeast near the intersection of Ninth Street and North Grand Avenue. Some buildings that were part of old Illinois Watch Factory are in the central part of the Sangamo complex. The old city reservoir and the lagoon in Reservoir Park can be seen in the upper right. *Courtesy Sangamon Valley Collection, Lincoln Library*

ABOVE: View of Fifth Street looking south from Adams Street, 1939.
Courtesy Sangamon Valley Collection, Lincoln Library

TOP LEFT: A bird's-eye view of Capitol Avenue looking west from Sixth Street, circa 1938.
Courtesy Sangamon Valley Collection, Lincoln Library

OPPOSITE: Aerial view of Springfield, circa 1937. *Courtesy Sangamon Valley Collection, Lincoln Library*

BELOW: A bird's-eye view of Monroe Street from Fifth Street, circa 1936.
Courtesy Sangamon Valley Collection, Lincoln Library

BELOW: View of 210-14 South Fifth Street, circa 1939.
Courtesy Sangamon Valley Collection, Lincoln Library

Transportation

Springfield didn't get its first motor car until 1901. Those early automobiles were loud, smelly and dangerous — Springfield's first car accident apparently happened in Washington Park in 1902 — but they also were fascinating and fashionable. Car owners posed proudly for photographs in their new acquisitions, even if — as in the case of Dr. W.P. Armstrong in 1909 (p.19) — they had to do so in freezing weather, protected by a woolen cloak, fur lap robe and bowler hat.

Less prosperous residents got around town via electric streetcars, which were cheap and reliable — though not foolproof. "Babies are rare finds on streetcars," the Illinois State Journal reported, reassuringly, in 1928. "Only one case of a mother forgetting her offspring has been reported within the last few years."

If central Illinoisans needed to travel out of town, they were likely to take advantage of what everybody called "the interurban." The Illinois Traction System operated a 550-mile network of electrically powered trains throughout most of downstate Illinois from the early 1900s into the 1950s. Interurban trains — quiet, fast, frequent, even luxurious — connected whistle stops and farming hamlets to communities as large as Springfield, Peoria and St. Louis.

"The local trains stopped at all the road crossings — they were sometimes marked on telephone poles — and picked people up," former interurban worker Ray Reed of Chatham remembered for a State Journal-Register story in 2001. "If some farmer wanted to go into town on a Friday night to sell his eggs, he could do that. Then he could turn around and catch the first train home."

LEFT: Carl Meyer out for a drive, circa 1915. *Courtesy Dorothy Ewing*

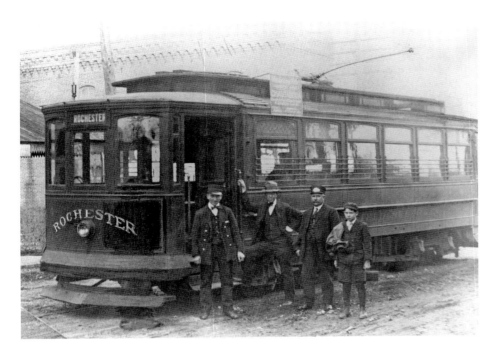

ABOVE: First day of operation, Springfield, Clearlake and Rochester Interurban Railroad line, car No. 48. June 10, 1908. This line lasted until July 1912. *Courtesy Robert Fairchild*

ABOVE: Early Studebaker Commander four-door sedan. *Courtesy Sangamon Valley Collection, Lincoln Library*

LEFT: Illinois Traction System station, early 1900s. *Courtesy Sangamon Valley Collection, Lincoln Library*

OPPOSITE: Unidentified women out for a drive in front of the Governor's Mansion, circa 1908. *Courtesy Sangamon Valley Collection, Lincoln Library*

BELOW: Gamma Club automobile tour in the spring of 1912. *Courtesy Jean S. Chase*

ABOVE: Springfield streetcar, circa 1912. *Courtesy Sangamon Valley Collection, Lincoln Library*

BELOW: C & A Railroad stop near a water tower, 1914. Third from left is Joseph Stublefield. *Courtesy Joanne Hott*

ABOVE: In 1915, the Paige Touring car was a stylish way to get around town. Notice the people in the back seat are playing checkers. They are at Washington Park. *Courtesy J.D. (Jim) Allen*

BELOW: James Dalbey with his daughter, Araminta, in the driver's seat of his car, circa 1912. *Courtesy David Dalbey*

ABOVE: Wabash Railroad passenger station located at 10th and Washington streets until it was destroyed by fire in the late 1930s. Photo circa 1918. *Courtesy Hubert Walton*

TOP: Frank J. Mueller, Johnette Maisenbacher Mueller Verardi, Mercedes Maisenbacher Mueller McHugh and Anna Marie Maisenbacher Mueller take a rest on the running board of their touring car, circa 1918. *Courtesy Nancy McHugh Hahn*

TOP LEFT: Crowd gathers as the Overland automobile makes its way to Springfield during an endurance run, circa 1917. *Courtesy Sangamon Valley Collection, Lincoln Library*

BOTTOM LEFT: Mazrim brothers posing in an early vehicle, circa 1919. *Courtesy James R. McIntyre Jr.*

ABOVE: C.M. Fergo, statement clerk at Railway Express office, 1920s. *Courtesy Paul W. Mueller*

OPPOSITE: A streetcar and automobile share the road at the corner of Walnut Street and South Grand Avenue in 1925. Laurel United Methodist Church forms the backdrop of this scene. *Courtesy Albert C. Maurer*

BELOW: Chicago and Alton Railroad, 1926. The railroad was purchased by the Baltimore and Ohio Railroad in 1931. *Courtesy Sangamon Valley Collection, Lincoln Library*

ABOVE: Charles Lindbergh delivers the first airmail to Springfield, April 15, 1926. *Courtesy Sangamon Valley Collection, Lincoln Library*

BELOW: Ann Stroble sitting on Jim Ealey's coal delivery truck on Wesley Street, circa 1929. *Courtesy Joyce Stroble Stuper*

ABOVE: Advertisement for Springfield Auto Supply Company (SASCO) on the side of this airplane at Southwest Airport, circa 1930. *Courtesy Sangamon Valley Collection, Lincoln Library*

BELOW: Gainer Feeds and Schafer & Sons delivery truck, 1930s. *Courtesy Sharon Schafer Kording*

ABOVE: The Iso-Vis Motor Oil test car, that ran 9,000 miles on the Indianapolis Speedway, stopped off in Springfield on its cross-country tour October 31, 1931. Pictured, from left are, Frank J. Robinson, J.F. Dodson, salesmen for ArtRay Motor Co.; S. Seeman, driver of the car; A.S. Johnson, manager of ArtRay Motor Co.; Ray Johnson, assistant manager; Lee Havey, service manager. Charles F. Eberle of the Standard Oil company is in the background. *Courtesy Sangamon Valley Collection, Lincoln Library*

TOP: Gustav "Gus" Dudda outside his shop in a racing car he built, 1931. Gustav built a double overhead cam engine that raced in the Illinois and Indiana area in the early 1930s. The Dudda engine was developed using either a Chrysler or Plymouth block. *Courtesy Linda Dudda Dickerson and Alfred Dudda*

ABOVE: Riders on the last streetcar in Springfield, December 31, 1937. The following day, buses provided public transportation. *Courtesy Marlene Seaborn*

TOP: Last streetcar in Springfield, December 31, 1937. Charles S. "Bob" Seaborn, was the driver and he is standing next to the car. *Courtesy Marlene Seaborn*

TOP LEFT: Dr. W.B. Armstrong Jr. in his new Chrysler Roadster with sister and brother-in-law in front and three nephews in back. *Courtesy Charles Chapin*

BOTTOM LEFT: Fleet of new Checker Cabs, circa 1939. Frank Sgro owned the Allied Cab Company/Checker Cabs from about 1929 through 1942. *Courtesy Mary Frances Squires*

Commerce

In contrast to today's chain stores, discounters and big-box outlets, early Springfield commerce revolved around homegrown entrepreneurs. The window display at the first Mel-O-Cream Donut store (p. 53) hints at the secret of the Grant family's early success — donuts were fresh-baked twice daily, and you could satisfy your craving for a fresh glazed (or any of 15 other varieties) until midnight every night.

Paris Cleaners (also still run by its founding family, the Frankes), used superstition as one of its marketing gimmicks — Paris' early telephone number, Capitol 13, the company declared (p.55), was "Unlucky for Spots."

Many of the businesses chronicled in this section, are long gone of course — even such stalwarts as the Franklin Life Insurance Co., whose office workers posed for a few carefully staged photos (pp. 34-35) in the early 1900s. Gone, but not always forgotten — Ben Franklin's statue still sits outside what is now Illinois State Police headquarters.

LEFT: Capitol 24 Tire Co. employees, 1927. The shop was at 208-210 North Sixth Street. *Courtesy Sangamon Valley Collection, Lincoln Library*

29

ABOVE: Melvin's Drug Store at Fifth and Washington streets, 1865.
Courtesy Sangamon Valley Collection, Lincoln Library

RIGHT: Fogarty Bros. fine grocery store, 1890. The windows give a hint into the products this store carried; whiskey and brandy from California. Those known, from left are John G. Fogarty, unidentified, Tom J. Fogarty and the others are unidentified.
Courtesy Sangamon Valley Collection, Lincoln Library

BELOW: Myers Brothers Clothing Co. store, on the west side of the public square, circa 1886. *Courtesy Sangamon Valley Collection, Lincoln Library*

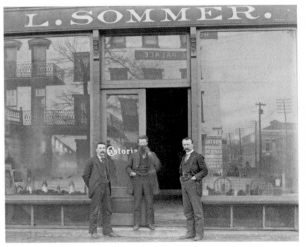

ABOVE: Dr. Louis Xavier Sommer & Sons drug store, 400 East Washington Street, 1875. His sons were Henry and Louis Jr. The reflections in the glass show the old City Hall building across the street. *Courtesy Mary L.W. Midden*

ABOVE: Henson Robinson Co. on Fifth Street, 1893. From left are George G. Wood, Edward G. Hofferkamp, Charles H. Robinson, George Murray, Henson Robinson, Adam Davis, and Jas Marley. *Courtesy Henson Robinson*

BELOW: Central Illinois Public Service Company ice delivery wagon and two employees in the early 1900s. The man at left with tongs is Charles G. Sutton. *Courtesy Nancy Hobbs*

ABOVE: Fritz Saloon at Sixth Street and North Grand Avenue, circa 1900. This was one of Fritz Maisenbacher's many enterprises. Fritz is the short man in front of the door. *Courtesy Nancy M. Hahn*

BELOW: Springfield Marine Bank on Sixth Street, circa 1895. In the photo are Jim Cook, Shelby Darwin, Ben Brainard and Henry Bunn. *Courtesy Sangamon Valley Collection, Lincoln Library*

ABOVE: C.A. Gehrmann, dealer in dry goods and millinery, was located at 113 South Fifth Street, circa 1901. *Courtesy Sangamon Valley Collection, Lincoln Library*

RIGHT: Paul and E. Redeker's wallpaper and paint business at 413 East Monroe Street, 1902. *Courtesy Sangamon Valley Collection, Lincoln Library*

FAR RIGHT: Standing in front of the old Paye Sporting Goods store in 1903 are, left to right, J. Lin Roll, bookkeeper; Theodore Bensen, delivery boy; Martin V. Troy, clerk; and James O'Brien, clerk. The store was located between Fourth and Fifth streets on Monroe Street and was one of Springfield's prominent business establishments. The window at the left displays an array of boxing gloves, fishing tackle, shotguns, small arms ammunition and punching bags. William Payne operated the store until his death in 1911, when Troy took over the business. The store dated back to 1858 when it was established by William Payne's father, Francis E. Payne. *Courtesy Sangamon Valley Collection, Lincoln Library*

ABOVE: Frank Wellman's cigar factory at 211 South Sixth Street, circa 1900s. *Courtesy Sangamon Valley Collection, Lincoln Library*

OPPOSITE: Gottschalk's Grocery at Edwards Street at College Street, March 8, 1898. *Courtesy Sangamon Valley Collection, Lincoln Library*

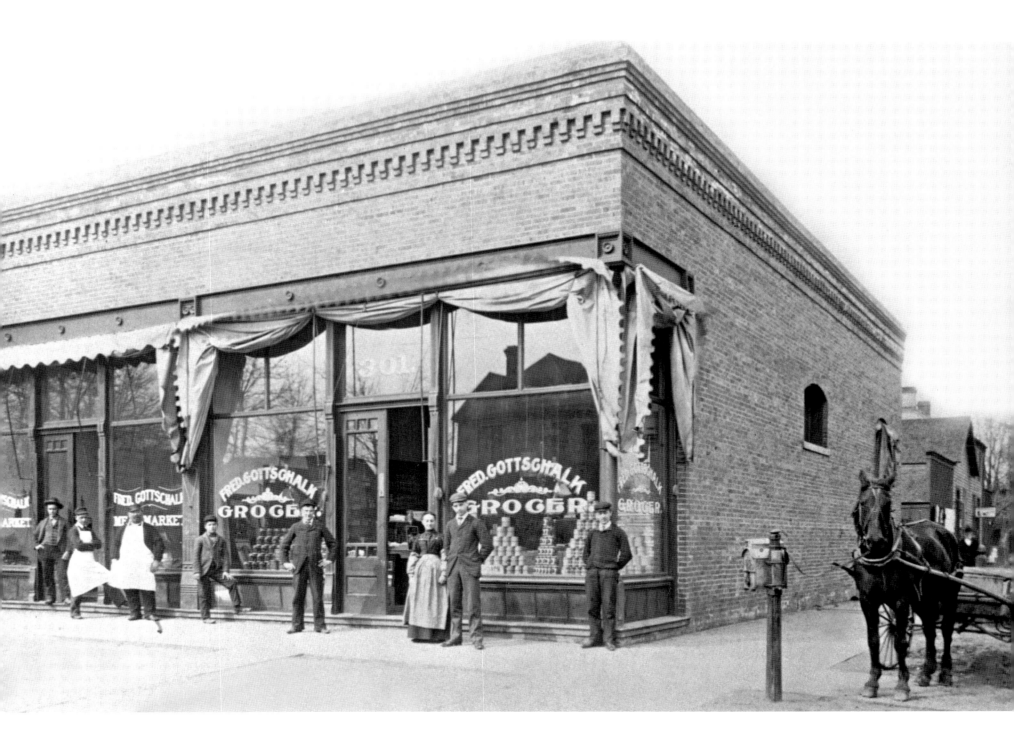

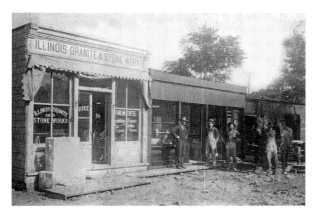

ABOVE: Illinois Granite and Stone Works at Third and Monroe streets, circa 1905. The owner, Henry Flynn, is at left.
Courtesy Margie Sheehan-Richards

ABOVE: Exterior of C.C. Troxell and J.T. Wright's business that sold farm machinery, leather goods and harnesses.
Courtesy Sangamon Valley Collection, Lincoln Library

TOP LEFT: Interior of grocery store owned by Mr. and Mrs. Henry Midden Sr., at Spring and Cook streets in 1904. Mrs. Midden Sr. operated this store after Henry passed away in 1928. The store stood at the site of the later Ideal Drug Store. *Courtesy Mary L.W. Midden*

LEFT: Interior of Franklin Life Insurance Co., early 1900s.
Courtesy Sangamon Valley Collection, Lincoln Library

OPPOSITE: Dr. Oscar F. Maxon, physician, and Mary L. Ross, stenographer, at the offices of Franklin Life Insurance Co., early 1900s. *Courtesy Sangamon Valley Collection, Lincoln Library*

ABOVE: Interior of James Ingels bicycle repair shop at 315 East Adams Street, circa 1909. *Courtesy Sangamon Valley Collection, Lincoln Library*

TOP RIGHT: The Clarkson and Mitchell drug store on the southwest corner of Fifth and Monroe streets, circa 1905. The soda fountain was a gathering spot for many Springfield folks. *Courtesy Sangamon Valley Collection, Lincoln Library*

BOTTOM RIGHT: Gelhard Riechs meat market at 217 North Fifth Street, circa 1905. *Courtesy Sangamon Valley Collection, Lincoln Library*

OPPOSITE: Henry Klintworth's Bar at 1231 East Cook Street, circa 1909. Henry's sons Henry, left, and George, with their pet billy goat. The two boys would attach a harness from the goat to a wagon and deliver groceries and kegs of beer. *Courtesy Jack Klintworth*

BELOW: Springfield's first cash-and-carry meat market, introduced by A.C. Connor, 1907. The market was at 628 East Washington Street. The site was later occupied by the Furniture Mart. From left are A.C. Connor, Howard Nateon, Harvey Connor, Mable Worthington, Julius Schlauber, Joe Englehart and Mr. Cadwallader. *Courtesy Sangamon Valley Collection, Lincoln Library*

ABOVE: Haenig Electric company, early 1910s. Frank Bishop is the only one identified and he is standing in the doorway. *Courtesy Sangamon Valley Collection, Lincoln Library*

RIGHT: Golden Rule Grocery, circa 1910. *Courtesy Randy von Liski*

BELOW: Springfield News carrier force when the old Springfield News was located on Adams Street, 1910. Included in the photo are Lawrence Head, "Dutch" Sternaman, Billy Knox, Dr. Donelan, Dr. Leslie Lambert, Stuart Reid, Frank Reid, Charles Kepner and Jimmie Row. *Courtesy Sangamon Valley Collection, Lincoln Library*

ABOVE: The Meyerhoff & Offer store on Carpenter Street between Seventh and Eighth streets, circa 1912. Owner Edwin Meyerhoff is holding the horse and his partner Frank Offer is in the wagon.
Courtesy Judy Reynolds

TOP: Interior of Henry Klintworth's Bar at 1231 East Cook Street, circa 1911. Judging from the stains on the floor, saloon patrons apparently had difficulty hitting the spittoon. The ad on the rear wall is for Reisch Beer, which was made in Springfield. *Courtesy Jack Klintworth*

LEFT: Exterior of J.T. O'Neil's at 1114 South Grand Avenue East, circa 1910.
Courtesy Sangamon Valley Collection, Lincoln Library

ABOVE: Customers getting their shoes shined at J.P "Jimmy" James shoe shine parlor, circa 1915. The business was in the Lincoln-Herndon Building. *Courtesy Jim Lutz*

RIGHT: Anton Zanders, right, and employee Arnold Boeltcher in front of Zanders Meat Market at 709 North 14th Street, circa 1913. *Courtesy Eileen (Zanders) Morris*

ABOVE: Youngsters who delivered papers on their bicycles for the Illinois State Journal and Illinois State Register, circa 1917. J. Richard Kaylor is the boy on the far right. Kaylor was born in 1910. *Courtesy Diane (Kaylor) Barghouti-Hardwick*

LEFT: Produce display in the window of the Ellis Briggs McAtee Grocery store, circa 1915. The store was located on North Sixth Street across from Ss. Peter and Paul Catholic Church. *Courtesy Michalene McAtee, Judy Gaye Brian and Kathy Beaver*

FAR LEFT: Frances (Burger) Hendricks behind the counter at Amrhein's Bakery at Eighth Street and North Grand Avenue in 1917. *Courtesy Frances (Hendricks) Loew*

ABOVE: Smith Grocery store at 716 North Grand Avenue West, circa 1920. *Courtesy Steve Mihelsic*

TOP MIDDLE: Marie (Carrico) Castor in front of the original Castor's Grocery Store, opened in 1915. William E. Castor Sr. is in the window. Photo, circa 1920. *Courtesy Bill Castor*

TOP RIGHT: Interior of Meador Electric at 408 East Adams Street, circa 1920. From left, Carroll Jones, Charles A. Meador (owner), and William R. Schnirring Sr. Mr. Schnirring purchased the company in 1929 and changed the name to Springfield Electric in 1932. *Courtesy William R. Schnirring*

BOTTOM RIGHT: Armstrong Bros. sheet-metal business at 713 East Adams Street, circa 1920. The business was run by brothers Harry and John Armstrong and E.G. George.
Courtesy Pat Kienzler

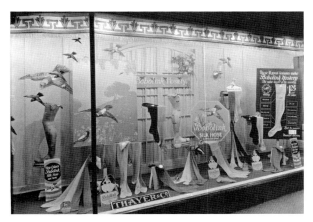

TOP: Sangamon Dairy horse-drawn milk wagons and drivers lined up in front of the dairy at Eighth and Monroe streets, 1923. The dairy was founded in 1910 by James A. Hall and William Wineteer. *Courtesy Sangamon Valley Collection, Lincoln Library*

MIDDLE LEFT: Thayer & Co. window display.
Courtesy Sangamon Valley Collection, Lincoln Library

BOTTOM LEFT: Interior of the first James Confectionery on South Grand Avenue between Sixth and Seventh streets, 1923.
Courtesy Jim Lutz

BOTTOM RIGHT: Myers Brothers Clothing Co. store at 406 1/2 Fifth Street. The first Myers store was in Athens, Ill., and was founded in 1858 by Morris Myers, an immigrant from Germany. The store was moved to Springfield in 1865. It was sold in 1873, the sons, Albert and Louis, being too young to take over. Later the two brothers, having worked in clothing stores in Springfield, purchased a small store on the west side of the square from Samuel Rosenwalk, who selected the two brothers to succeed him, and loaned them the money to get started. Myers Brothers opened in 1886 on the east side of the square. (Mr. Rosenwald left Springfield to join in the business of his son, Julius, a partner in Sears Roebuck.) In 1900, the business had expanded so greatly that a new five-story building was erected at the southwest corner of Fifth and Washington streets. Myers Brothers occupied two floors and the basement, business and professional offices occupied the remainder. The building was destroyed by fire the night of March 24, 1924. The Myers brothers made history by opening the business the following day, having purchased the stock and equipment of B.A. Lange Store. Here they conducted business while their new one-story building was completed. They closed at the Lange location on Saturday night, September 6, 1925, and opened in their new building on Tuesday September 8, 1925. In 1968, Myers announced a merger with the Phillips-Van Heusen Corporation of New York City. In 1978, Phillips-Van Heusen sold the Myers operation to P.A. Bergner of Peoria, and in 1982, the name "Myers Brothers" was replaced by Bergner's. *Courtesy Sangamon Valley Collection, Lincoln Library*

ABOVE: O'Shea Bros. Building Contractors truck "Ralph" (note "Ralph" painted on the truck), 1923. Glen Rose Woodland and Ralph G. O'Shea in front of her parents' (James and Susan Woodland) house at 1501 Edwards Street. Ralph and James O'Shea started the O'Shea Construction Company and later, Harold, a third brother, joined the business. *Courtesy Nancy Durbin*

TOP LEFT: Delivery truck for North End Bakery, also known as Knoedler's Bakery, located at 1131 North First Street, alongside the family home. It was owned and operated by Joseph and Helen Knoedler from 1911 to 1941. The motorized truck replaced the horse-drawn wagon. Seated on the running board are William and Henry, sons of Joseph and Helen. *Courtesy Helen Knoedler Maggiore*

BOTTOM LEFT: A.W. Sikking Co. at 213 North Sixth Street, 1920s. This store sold toys, appliances, hardware, housewares, musical instruments, televisions, radios and other goods. Notice the Justice of the Peace and Roma Italian and American restaurant on the second floor. *Courtesy Sangamon Valley Collection, Lincoln Library*

OPPOSITE: Springfield Auto Supply Company (SASCO) original store, 1926. Those known are Bill Menghini, founder of the business; Jack Brown, George England and Don Vance. Bill Menghini was also the founder of MENCO Corp. as well as the driving force behind the 87-warehousing network of Pronto auto parts distributors. SASCO was at one time a 12-outlet chain of auto parts stores. When Menghini was 21, he used his experience gained in high school to open an auto sub-dealership for Willys-Overland and Packard vehicles in 1925. He then convinced his employer, Albert Reisch of the brewery family, to spin off an auto parts business and it was named SASCO. In 1934, Menghini completed buying out Reisch and the business continued to grow to the point where MENCO and SASCO operations moved to the 200 block of East Washington Street. *Courtesy Sangamon Valley Collection, Lincoln Library*

ABOVE: William D. Stewart in front of Northside Food Shop at 801 1/2 North Grand Avenue East, circa 1926. W.H. Good, from whom Mr. Stewart purchased the store, is in the background. Mr. Stewart owned the store until his death in 1952. His grandchildren and great-grandchildren continue to live in the Springfield area. *Courtesy Peggy Buecker*

TOP RIGHT: Springfield Produce Co. delivery wagon, 1930s. Notice the sign advertising National Apple Week. *Courtesy Sangamon Valley Collection, Lincoln Library*

BOTTOM RIGHT: The Orpheum Theater in the late 1920s. *Courtesy Sangamon Valley Collection, Lincoln Library*

OPPOSITE TOP: Fleet of cars in front of Hotel Abraham Lincoln available for rent or purchase from Capital Drive Yourself Co. *Courtesy Sangamon Valley Collection, Lincoln Library*

OPPOSITE BOTTOM: Hotel Abraham Lincoln staff members, 1928. The hotel was at Fifth Street and Capitol Avenue. *Courtesy Janet Q. Davis*

Hotel ABRAHAM LINCOLN

ABOVE: Interior of Ritter Barber Shop at 300 East Washington Street (south side), 1930. *Courtesy Robert Ritter*

BELOW: Interior of American Shoe Shop at 227 East Monroe Street, circa 1930. George Coldewey, owner, is in the center. *Courtesy Margaret Egan and Sarah Hulsen*

ABOVE: Composing room workers hard at their craft at the Illinois State Journal, circa 1930. *Courtesy Sangamon Valley Collection, Lincoln Library*

BELOW: Electric Motor Shop at 803-805 East Jefferson Street, circa 1929. *Courtesy Jack D. Irving*

ABOVE: Sears, Roebuck and Co. sold bicycles as seen in this photo that was taken in the 1930s. A great way to display the bicycles was to put them out on the sidewalk in front of the store at 621 East Adams Street. *Courtesy Sangamon Valley Collection, Lincoln Library*

RIGHT: James R. McIntyre Sr. at his service station at Seventh and Jefferson streets, circa 1932. *Courtesy James R. McIntyre Jr.*

BOTTOM LEFT: Interior of S.M.W. Auto Supply at 326 North Sixth Street, 1931. William M. Stowell is on the right and his employee Amos E. Allen is on the left. The business was established in 1921 by William Stowell, Alfred Mills and Carlin Whittaker at 430 South Fourth Street, moving to 326 North Sixth Street in 1931. In 1944, it moved to its present location at 100 West Jefferson Street. Amos Allen began working for S.M.W. in 1928 for $12 a week. During the Depression, he was paid with a sewing machine by a customer. (The family still owns the sewing machine.) Allen became sole owner in 1955 and his daughter, Betty Hart, in 1979. S.M.W. stocked parts for Model-Ts, tires, batteries, brake shoes, belts and paint. Some of the products have been used in Springfield in a most unique way: numbering pigs and colorful hats at the Illinois State Fair, on the water slide and in restoration of the Old State Capitol building. *Courtesy Betty Hart*

BELOW: Hartmann Bakery at Ninth and Washington streets. Lottie Guygett, the "midget" atop the truck and Robert Wadlow, 8-feet, 11-inches tall, from Alton, is the tallest man in the crowd. Norbert Lemons is the man in the white suit to the left of the "giant." *Courtesy Sharon, Arolyn and Stephanie Lemons*

ABOVE: "Budweiser Girls" employed by the brewery touting Budweiser Beer sold at Schafer Distributor Co. after the repeal of prohibition, circa 1934. "Girls will live on diet of beer." *Courtesy Sangamon Valley Collection, Lincoln Library*

BELOW: Interior of Home Appliance Corp. store at Sixth Street and Capitol Avenue across from Leland Hotel in the 1930s. The man at far left is Luther Burbank. The woman in the photo is Bernice Stoner. *Courtesy William A. Denham*

ABOVE: Employees of Motor Inn at Fourth and Monroe streets, 1934. Edward Landholt is third from right and Richard Landholt is second from right. *Courtesy Margaret C. Landholt and Laura Landholt*

BELOW: Employees and the owner of Motor Inn, a storage garage at Fourth and Monroe streets, 1933. It was in business for 65-70 years. Owner, Ed Richter is in the middle of the back row. Gilbert Dietrich, manager, is second from the right in the front row. *Courtesy John Dietrich*

ABOVE: Men's department staff, Myers Brothers Clothing Co., 1936. The men's department was on the second floor. Vice-president Bill Meteen is in the second row, third man from the left. To his right is Stanley Myers, general manager of the store. *Courtesy Louis Myers Family*

BELOW: People gather at Joe Schafer Poultry Supplies in the 1930s. *Courtesy Sharon Schafer Kording*

ABOVE: Standard gas station at 1923 East Clearlake Avenue in the 1930s. John "Pop" Miller was in charge of this station for more than 38 years. The station was located in front of the Standard Oil bulk plant, across the street from Bianco's Little Supper Club. The station closed in 1968. *Courtesy Robert Johnson*

BOTTOM LEFT: Workers inside Amrhein's Bakery, circa 1935. *Courtesy Mary Midden*

BELOW: Employees and owners of the Alvin Krell Co., shortly before the company moved from 918 East Jefferson Street to a new building at 808 East Jefferson Street, circa 1937. From left, Alfred Cizauckas, Phil Grieme, Jack Kornfield, Jerome Seiz, Walter Sembell, Martha Jorgensen, Bertha, Alvin Jr., and Alvin Krell Sr. *Courtesy Marjorie and Alvin Krell Jr.*

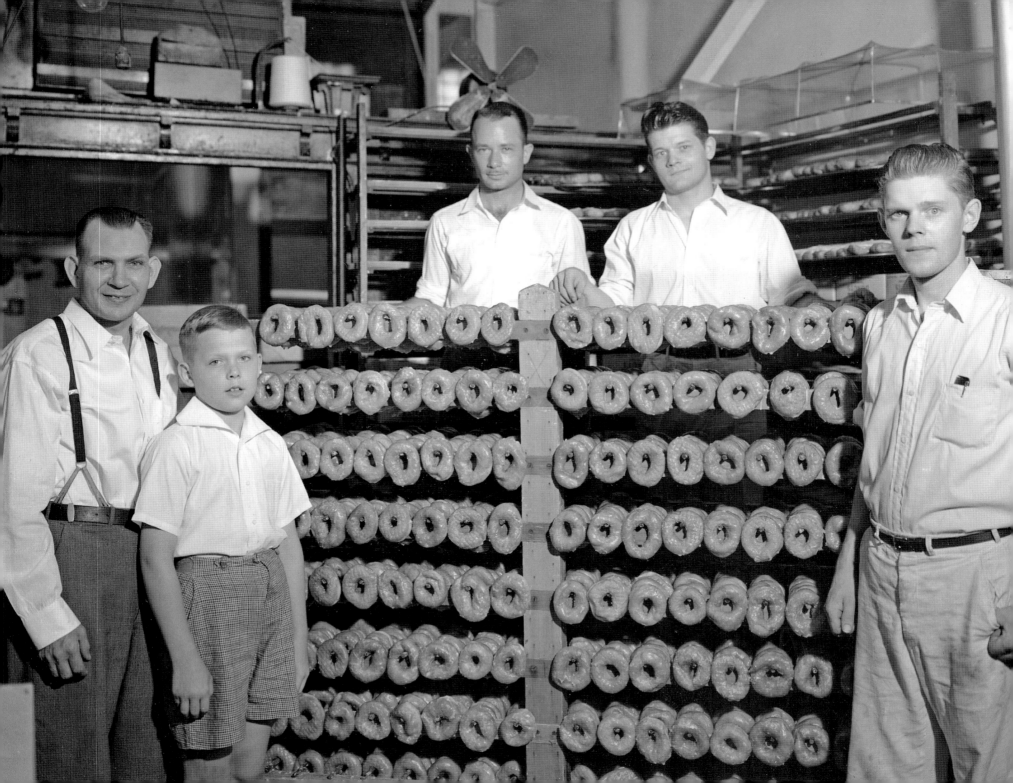

ABOVE: The start of construction of the Illinois Bell Telephone Company building at the corner of Sixth and Cook streets, April 11, 1938. *Courtesy Don Evans, Evans Construction*

OPPOSITE: The original Mel-O-Cream Donuts shop at 219 East Jefferson Street in 1938. From left, founding owner of the shop, Kelly Grant; his son, Kelly Jr., 9, current chairman of the board of Mel-O-Cream Donuts International, Inc.; Herschel Black, head sales clerk; George Gramlich, head baker; and Eddie Sassenberger, donut fryer. *Courtesy Kelly Grant Jr.*

BELOW: John Shea shows off his new cutting block in front of his meat market at 1100 South 11th Street, circa 1938. *Courtesy Jack Klintworth*

ABOVE: Front window of the original Mel-O-Cream Donuts shop at 219 East Jefferson Street in 1938. Note the glazed donuts at the time of this photo sold for 25 cents a dozen. *Courtesy Kelly Grant Jr.*

BELOW: The South Town Theatre at 1106 South Grand Avenue East, circa 1938. *Courtesy Craig Ewing*

ABOVE: Bicyclists line up in front of D.B. Hodge Tire Co. at 622 South Spring Street, circa 1936. Mr. Hodge is credited with opening the first super-service station in Springfield. He initially opened a small store at Spring and Cook streets in 1920 and his business grew to the point where he moved to a bigger location across the street in 1922. In 1923, Mr. Hodge purchased the entire corner on the northeast corner of Spring and Cook streets. *Courtesy Sagamon Valley Collection, Lincoln Library*

MIDDLE: Edward H. Richter & Sons meat market at 501 Sixth Street, 1920s. *Courtesy Nancy (Richter) Lashbrook, David Richter and Janet Richter*

BOTTOM RIGHT: Fred Smith in front of Handy Andy which was located at Ninth and Washington streets, 1925. Fred Smith went on to open and manage several A&P Grocery stores in Springfield. *Courtesy Humphrey's Market/Hope Humphrey-Wallace*

FAR RIGHT: Joe Hartman when he was a meat cutter with Piggly Wiggly on South Grand Avenue, 1939. *Courtesy Rich Hartman*

OPPOSITE: For many years, trucks and delivery equipment of Paris Cleaners carried the slogan "Unlucky for Spots." This photo taken March 19, 1930, substantiates that "13" over the years, has been "unlucky for spots," but indeed lucky for Paris Cleaners. The cleaning firm was established in 1909 by Carl D. Franke Sr. Those indentified are, from left, Guy Morris, Dewey Blaine, two unidentified, Bert Hopkins, Vern McGraw, unidentified motorcyclist, and Louis A. Crawford. Mr. Crawford later operated the Crawford Cycle Shop. *Courtesy Sangamon Valley Collection, Lincoln Library*

Industry

Springfield is a white- and pink-collar town today, but that's a relatively new development. Well within living memory, local laborers' collars were much more likely to be blue or — considering central Illinois' coal-mining heritage — often black.

The first Sangamon County mines opened in 1866. By the 1890s, the county was the second-highest-producing coal county in Illinois, and Illinois ranked behind only Pennsylvania for coal production among states. The mines drew laborers to central Illinois from around the world — Irish, Italians, Germans, Lithuanians and many others. It was a tough life, and it brewed tough people. One of the toughest, legendary United Mine Workers of America president John L. Lewis, lived in Springfield and is buried in Oak Ridge Cemetery.

Factory jobs were plentiful, too, at Springfield Iron Co., the Springfield Woolen Mills and the A.L. Ide &

Sons (manufacturer of the innovative Ide Steam Engine) in early Springfield, and later at Allis-Chalmers/Fiatallis, Weaver Manufacturing and Pillsbury Mills. (When, as a gimmick, Pillsbury once paid all its workers in silver dollars, paymasters were guarded by both uniformed police officers and plainclothes guards bearing tommy guns. See p.64.)

Cleaner working conditions — and, by the photographic evidence, good jobs for women — were available at the Illinois Watch Co., which filled a demand for super-accurate "railroad watches," and its cousin the Sangamo Electric Co. Sangamo (p. 65), which specialized in electric meters, remained one of the city's biggest manufacturers well into the 1970s.

LEFT: Wirth & Gaupp Northside Greenhouse employees at 1107 North First Street, circa 1908. *Courtesy Sangamon Valley Collection, Lincoln Library*

ABOVE: A.L. Ide with his Ide Steam Engine, circa 1880. Mr. Ide started the first electrical power company in Springfield and provided the first electric lights around the town square. Mr. Ide also was engaged in the steam heating business and was awarded the contract for the heating systems in the new State Capitol building in 1870. Ide was one of Springfield's most successful inventors and manufacturers and gained a world-wide reputation for his design, construction and perfecting the high-speed automatic steam engine.
Courtesy Yvonne Butcher

ABOVE: Springfield Woolen Mills on the east side of Fourth Street between Capitol Avenue and Jackson Street, circa 1878. This Springfield industry was the outgrowth of a wool carding business started in 1834 by H.M. Armstrong and John Dryer.
Courtesy Sangamon Valley Collection, Lincoln Library

BOTTOM LEFT: Observatory of the Illinois Watch Co., manufacturers of the celebrated Bunn Special, Sangamo Special and A. Lincoln railroad watches. In this observatory, correct time was taken by transit observations of the stars. This was checked by daily wireless signals from the National Wireless Station in Arlington, Va. *Courtesy Sangamon Valley Collection, Lincoln Library*

BELOW: Illinois Watch Co. factory building, 1890s.
Courtesy Debbie Barrow

ABOVE: Assembly room, Sangamo Electric Co., circa 1900. *Courtesy Debbie Barrow*

LEFT: Assembly room, Sangamo Electric Co., 1905. Uffie Wieties is in the second row by the window. The founders, R.C. Lanphier and J.H. Hodde, are in the background wearing vests and ties. *Courtesy Debbie Barrow*

BELOW: Illinois Watch Co. factory workers, circa 1905. James H. Page is seen in the middle on the right. Charlotte Wirster Page also worked at the factory. *Courtesy June Rutherford*

ABOVE: Employees of Sangamo Electric Co., June 2, 1915. *Courtesy Sangamon Valley Collection, Lincoln Library*

LEFT: Two men looking at the axle on an automobile at Weaver Manufacturing, circa 1920. The company was in the 2100 block of South Ninth Street, and made auto lifts and jacks. *Courtesy Verna Cutler*

OPPOSITE MIDDLE LEFT: Starnes Shaft No. 1, three miles east of Springfield, circa 1889. *Courtesy Sangamon Valley Collection, Lincoln Library*

OPPOSITE BOTTOM LEFT: Employees of the Illinois Watch Co. factory hard at work, circa 1915. *Courtesy Sangamon Valley Collection, Lincoln Library*

OPPOSITE RIGHT: Illinois Watch Co. train room employees, circa 1908. *Courtesy Sangamon Valley Collection, Lincoln Library*

BELOW: Construction of Pillsbury Mills, circa 1920. *Courtesy Sangamon Valley Collection, Lincoln Library*

ABOVE: Workers from Weaver Manufacturing working on a car, March 14, 1927. *Courtesy Dave Goriszewski and Sharon Gipson*

BELOW: Springfield stock yard executives, circa 1926. From left, A.D. Van Meter, H.C. Harms, John Geoff, George Bell and I.A. Madden. *Courtesy Yolanda Bastas*

ABOVE: Inspection party from Powell Garard and Co., Chicago, at Union Fuel Co. property, October 22, 1921. *Courtesy Sangamon Valley Collection, Lincoln Library*

BELOW: American Radiator Co., circa 1928. This view is looking north from East Ash Street between Yale Boulevard and 14th Street. *Courtesy Sangamon Valley Collection, Lincoln Library*

ABOVE: Pillsbury Mill, circa 1930. *Courtesy Sangamon Valley Collection, Lincoln Library*

BELOW: Allis-Chalmers Manufacturing Co. plant, circa 1930. *Courtesy Sangamon Valley Collection, Lincoln Library*

ABOVE: Allis-Chalmers Manufacturing Co. machine shop workers, 1932. *Courtesy Sangamon Valley Collection, Lincoln Library*

BELOW: Coal mining was one of the big industries in the 1930s. *Courtesy Sangamon Valley Collection, Lincoln Library*

ABOVE: Silver Dollar Pay Week at Pillsbury Mills, 1930s. *Courtesy Sangamon Valley Collection, Lincoln Library*

RIGHT: Flag raising at Weaver Manufacturing in the 1930s. *Courtesy Bill Becker*

BELOW: Silver Dollar Pay Week at Pillsbury Mills, 1930s. *Courtesy Sangamon Valley Collection, Lincoln Library*

ABOVE: Conrad Griesser, brewmaster, stands beside the brew kettle (11,520 gallon capacity) at Reisch Brewery company, circa 1935. *Courtesy Sangamon Valley Collection, Lincoln Library*

OPPOSITE: Workers at Sangamo Electric Co., circa 1939. These workers are splitting mica to be used in the electric meters that Sangamo produced. Those included in the photo, from left, Doris Moore, unidentified, Beulah Buckhold, Betty Sullivan, Edna Dixen, Helen Ciota, Ann Becker, Marguerite (Hillen) Hager, and unidentified. Back row, first six unidentified, Mary Weiss, unidentified, Lorraine Neuby, Violet Grishes, Pauline McDougal, Ann Durako, Elsie Duda, and supervisor Irene Walsh (standing). *Courtesy Rita Moore*

BELOW: Employees of Schultz Bakery in 1938. *Courtesy Charles Gramlich*

Schools & Education

Stuart School was at Sixth and Vine streets in Springfield in 1915. Corralling some 200 or so grade-schoolers long enough for a photograph to be taken must have been quite a task. That makes the Stuart School photo an impressive tribute to the personality — and, probably, the disciplinary abilities, too — of Stuart School Principal Nellie Engelskirchen.

But the fact that Miss Engelskirchen thought the effort was worthwhile speaks to the value education was given in early Springfield, as do many of the other photos in this chapter. Graduation, whether from grade school or high school, was a milestone in the lives of central Illinois students and their families.

The Springfield High School Class of 1894, the Edwards School Class of 1903, the Ss. Peter and Paul School Class of '20, the Lincoln School Class of '25, the white-clad St. Joseph School Class of '33 … their descendants know these fresh-faced graduates only as parents or grandparents, if they know them at all. It's good to remember they were young once, too, and ready to take on the world.

LEFT: Students and faculty of Stuart School gather for a photo in front of their school building, circa 1915. *Courtesy Randy von Liski*

ABOVE: Buckhart Grade School students, circa 1895.
Courtesy Rochester Historical Preservation Society

BELOW: Crowd gathers for the laying of the cornerstone of Lincoln School, 1900. The school is at 11th Street and Capitol Avenue. *Courtesy Peg Kruger, Lincoln Magnet School*

ABOVE: Children on a school outing in 1890. Clarence Gum Lambert is at the front of the wagon with a dark bow tie. *Courtesy Rose Lambert*

BELOW: Springfield High School graduating class of 1894. *Courtesy Sangamon Valley Collection, Lincoln Library*

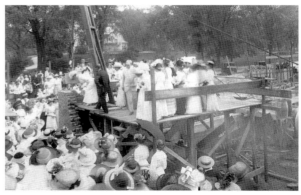

BELOW: Springfield High School Latin class, circa 1890. *Courtesy Sangamon Valley Collection, Lincoln Library*

ABOVE: Hay School at Henrietta and Lawrence avenues, circa 1901. *Courtesy Sangamon Valley Collection, Lincoln Library*

TOP LEFT: Springfield High School graduating class of 1900. *Courtesy Sangamon Valley Collection, Lincoln Library*

BOTTOM LEFT: Teachers of Sangamon County Rural and Village Schools, 1902. Wm. R. Cory later became a principal at Rochester School, principal of Dawson School and principal of other schools. The photo was taken on the steps of the Illinois State Capitol. *Courtesy Linda North Cox*

ABOVE: Students in front of Mt. Zion School in the early 1900s. The concrete steps still are in place at 4002 Mt. Zion School Road. They are the only thing left marking where the schoolhouse once stood. *Courtesy Robert Johnson*

TOP RIGHT: Hay School graduation class, 1906. Standing are John Ball, Adolph Deiken, Ella V. Hamilton (principal), Bessie Foraker, Raymond Renetzki and Arthur Herford. Middle row, Virginia Yates, Nona Doyle, Etta Thompson, Nina Kimmell and Douglas Gilbert. Front row, Delbert Duke, Albert Livingstone, unidentified and Harry Richardson. *Courtesy Sangamon Valley Collection, Lincoln Library*

BOTTOM RIGHT: Harvard Park School on the south side of Oberlin Avenue between 11th Street and Yale Boulevard, October 1912. *Courtesy Sangamon Valley Collection, Lincoln Library*

OPPOSITE: Edwards School eighth-grade graduating class, 1903. Pictured are Olive Reiger, Warren Colby, Miss Nanette Cotton, Grace Goveia, Willard Seekridge, Bertha Thompson, Alfleda Wormgood, Ellen Lucker, Hazel Bater, Edith Smith, Myrtle Cash, Anna Grace Hopkins, Fred Neal, Susie McCutcheon, Shelby McCoy, Lester Shaffer, George McCoy, Alex Schroeder, Harry Hoyt and Henry Richardson. The order of those identified is unknown. *Courtesy Sangamon Valley Collection, Lincoln Library*

ABOVE: Second-grade class at Converse School, circa 1915. *Courtesy David Dalbey*

TOP RIGHT: Springfield High School cooking class, circa 1912. *Courtesy Sangamon Valley Collection, Lincoln Library*

BOTTOM RIGHT: Iles Elementary School first-grade class in 1915. William E. Castor Sr., kneeling, fourth from the left, is in the front row. *Courtesy Bill Castor*

BELOW: Ss. Peter and Paul School graduates, 1920. *Courtesy Sangamon Valley Collection, Lincoln Library*

ABOVE: Independence School graduates in 1921. From left, back row, Beatrice Mayol, Mary Helen Winch and Mary Stroble. Front row, Dorothy Mcnabb and Elizabeth Staub. *Courtesy Marjorie and Alvin Krell Jr.*

BELOW: Ss. Peter and Paul School classroom, 1915. *Courtesy Sangamon Valley Collection, Lincoln Library*

ABOVE: Ss. Peter and Paul School eighth-grade graduates, 1923. *Courtesy Pat Ebel Dietrich*

BELOW: Sacred Heart Academy, first-grade class, 1922. This was a boarding school at the time of the photo. *Courtesy Clarissa Milligan Cullen*

ABOVE: Members of the first school patrol in Springfield, April 1927. The 107 boys took the oath led by Mayor J. Emil Smith. *Courtesy Sangamon Valley Collection, Lincoln Library*

ABOVE: Trinity Lutheran School classroom, circa 1926. Identified are Raymond Klein, Clara Clark, Louise Schmidt, Gretchen Heineman, Walter Werner, Paul Halter, Charles Beatty, Clarence Gross, Ernest Schmidt, Leona Stuemke, Margaret Clark, Catherine Siebert, Anita Bickhaus, Johanna Linton, Clara Jeglia, Margaret Coldewey, Emil Blase, Glen Mester, Arthur Roschanski, Walter Ladage, Dorothea Siebert, Rose Stoblers, Margaret Napinski, Marion Zund, Ann Friedmeyer, Helene Ostermieres, Carl Kuhlmann, Fred Kohles, Alfred Tansky, George Wendt, Elsie Zachery, Gertie Albrecht, Alice Rehwald, Anna Moskelevski, Evelyn Jacobs, Earnest Mack, George Ratz, Emil Mack, Walter Wendt, Helen Ploczika, Harold Coynes, Louise Augustine, Earnest Netznick, Gus Kopatz, Paris Polblinski, and Eddie Remack. The order of those identified is unknown. *Courtesy Margaret Egan and Sarah Hulsen*

RIGHT: Ridgely School graduating class of 1922. From left, first row, Margaret Churnis, Ogretta Farrand, Eunice Collard, Mary Morris, Amelia Laurick, Anna Stankavich, Jessie Adometis and Anna Andrish. Second row, Clara Kunz (teacher), Julia Patrick, Glenn Smith, Donald Cornish, Rene Arthur Suplit, Ira Aldrich, Lee Hodgson, Kyiat Serrtarous, Emil Blasek and Margaret Loda. Principal J.M. Humer is in the back. *Courtesy Fritzi Cartwright*

ABOVE: Kindergarten and first-grade classes at Converse School in 1925. The girl at the teacher's left is identified as Elora Hendricks. *Courtesy Marilyn Stalets*

LEFT: Eighth-grade classroom at Sacred Heart School, circa 1928. *Courtesy Dylan Shomidie*

BELOW: Blessed Sacrament School, eighth-grade graduation class, June 1930. Robert J. Christine is seen in front row, last boy on the right. *Courtesy Barbara Christine Morris*

Graduates
~1930~

LEFT: Lincoln School eighth-grade graduation class, 1925. D'Arcy Artis is fourth from left in the second row. Catherine Cothren is second from left in the third row; she later would teach school in District 186, Southeast High School. *Courtesy Joyce L. Beard*

OPPOSITE: Eighth-grade graduation at Ss. Peter and Paul School in 1930. *Courtesy Nancy Dillon*

BELOW: St. Joseph School graduating class, 1933. *Courtesy Dan Connolly*

ABOVE: Palmer School eighth-grade graduation, 1934. *Courtesy Tammy Taylor*

RIGHT: Enos School students, 1934. *Courtesy Ross Hendrickson*

OPPOSITE: Bunn School graduating class, June 1933. *Courtesy Sangamon Valley Collection, Lincoln Library*

BELOW: Iles School graduating class of 1934. *Courtesy Randy von Liski*

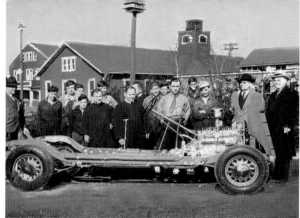

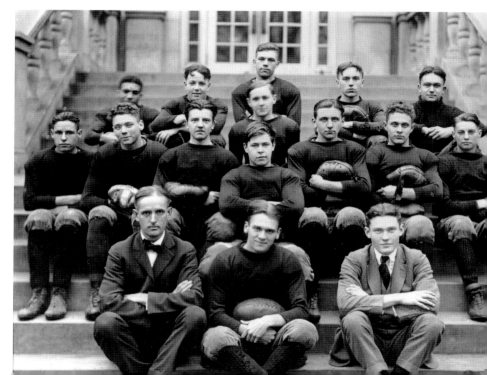

ABOVE: Harvard Park School graduating class, January 1937. *Courtesy Sangamon Valley Collection, Lincoln Library*

ABOVE: Springfield High School manual arts class, 1930s. *Courtesy Sangamon Valley Collection, Lincoln Library*

BOTTOM RIGHT: Lanphier High School's first basketball team, 1936–37. Players, from left, back row are G. Constantino, William Gabriel, R. Stevenson, H. Reisch and G. Stickney. Kneeling, D. Conavay, J. LaRocca, J. Fults and W. Emmons. Sitting is T. O'Reilly. The team was coached by Hugo Lindquist, who is to the far right. *Courtesy Sangamon Valley Collection, Lincoln Library*

BELOW: Butler School first-grade class, 1936. Identified are Janice Headrich, Tina Bartsokas, Jane Towler, Jean Majors, Sally Spaulding, Marjorie Spafford and Jack Williams. The order of those identified is unknown. *Courtesy Sangamon Valley Collection, Lincoln Library*

LEFT: Shorthand class at Lanphier High School in 1939.
Courtesy Frances (Hendricks) Loew

OPPOSITE: The first Lanphier High School football team, 1937. The coach was Don Anderson. His assistant was Cleo Dopp. Managers were Pete Maggio and Jack Myers. Among the players were Leon Petrilli (50), Jack Freeman (33), Lyle Coy (55), Robert Ayers (12), Fred Yannone (35), Louie Zanardi (25), Louis Flammini (37), and Wally Groesch (24). Also included in the photo are Ray Ramsey, Jack Trout, Don Jackson, Robert Brooks, Louis Gibbs and Ray Stevenson. The order of those identified is unknown. *Courtesy Louis J. Zanardi*

ABOVE: Lanphier High School graduating class of 1939. First row, Helen Sprouse, Bernice Rautis, Caroline Martin, Margaret Craig, Maurine Benson, Louise Nesbitt, Stella Saputo, Anna Shevokas, Sylvia Petrokas, Melba Cason, Pauline Fox, Hazel Betty, Catherine Bierbaum, Lucille Bierbusse, Norma Bollman, Jacqueline McCorkle, Betty George, Helen Peters, Betty Means, Eileen Ingram, Mildred Burns, Arlene Thompson, Geraldine Monahan, Margaret Kopatz, Ida Hurrelbrink, Concetta Benanti, and Rose Calandrino. Second row, Retha Redpath, Virginia Morris, Gilda Frasco, Lucille Bourgasser, Louise McCarthy, Elizabeth Krska, Anita Wieties, Esther Lazar, Virginia Ogez, Betty Lou Simpson, Betty Courtney, Elizabeth LeFevre, Catherine Plain, Mary Knight, Esther Klein, Helen Cornwell, Florence Jasmon, Mary Jane McDaniel, Helen Skoda, Mary Corsco, Muriel Alkire, Elizabeth Thomason, Marion Courtwright, Mary Hitt, Dorothy Coleman, Jane Wiedlocher, and Betty Yoggerst. Third row, Margaret Forgas, Ruth Kincaid, Frieda Roschanske, Marie Beck, Ellen Keen, Miriam Clinebell, Frances Ann Hendricks, Janette Hodge, Shirley Bolinger, Vergie Olds, and Catherine Campbell. Fourth row, John Hayes, Rinaldo DiRocco, Nick Frasco, Armin Groesch, Carl Schuerman, Albert Raulin, Harold Smith, John Williamson, Joe Lynch, Marvin Ross, Bud Whitmore, Stanley Wilde, Walter Naschinski, James Lascody, Dave Yuroff, Charles Thompson, Robert Waters, Jay Griswold, Levi Stine, Charles Strode, Arthur Kunz, and Ben Stillwagon. Fifth row, Ray Schneider, Edward Arn, Olen Smock, Donald Pickett, William Apblett, Frank Bowyer, Kenneth Register, Burton Jolley, Kenneth Schmeing, Robert Cantrall, Lyle Coy, Russell Gillock, Remus Favero, Louis Torretto, Arthur Netznik, Jack Bawulski, Bud Fernandes, Tom Maybury, Carl Kopatz Tom O'Reilly, James Whitlock, Jim Foster, James Miller, Harry Abbott, Lawrence DeFrates, and Francis Ermann. *Courtesy Frances (Hendricks) Loew*

Public Service

Horse-drawn fire engines, U.S. Mail buggies and an 1897 class of nursing students from the long-gone Springfield Hospital and Training School, wearing caps and long, demure skirts, seem quaint today. But two photos demonstrate that public service was a serious vocation in the Springfield of the past, as it remains today.

Under their antique helmets, the members of the 1918 Springfield Police Department seem uniformly stolid and serious (facing page). But one face stands out — that of the department's lone black officer. Maybe it's going too far for a viewer today to also read pride and determination in his anonymous gaze. But maybe it's not.

Tragedy is written across the face of the Rev. Dr. John Thomas (p. 93) as he leads the funeral procession of Sgt. Porter Williams, a Springfield police detective who was shot to death during a battle between rival mine unions in 1932. The Springfield Police Department today gives its annual Porter Williams Award to an officer who has demonstrated exceptional bravery.

LEFT: The Springfield Police Department, circa 1918.
Courtesy Norma J. Clayton

ABOVE: Members of the Springfield Police Department, circa 1889. Identified are Chief James Donelan; Sergeants William Johnson and Thomas O'Leary; policemen John McLean, Thomas McGrath, Mike McCoy, Edward Maher, William Crow, Joseph Garber, Jack Doyle, John Hutchinson, Adam Koch, Wyatt Johnson, Henry Zimmerman, George Eck, Val Steffan, Jesse Ankrom, John Maloney, Thomas McCaffery, and WIlliam Sheehan. The order of those indentified is unknown. *Courtesy Sangamon Valley Collection, Lincoln Library*

BELOW: Springfield firemen, circa 1890. Left to right, back row are Charles Phillips, Phillip Hoffman, August Miller, Chief R. Young, Chris Decker and John Freeman (who later died in Chicago Cold Storage plant fire during the Chicago World's Fair in 1893). Front row, Robert Peel, Henry Miller, Oscar Phillips, Evan T. Jones and Thomas Dunn. *Courtesy Sangamon Valley Collection, Lincoln Library*

ABOVE: Firemen from Firehouse No. 7 at Edwards and Walnut streets, 1890s. Wm. Simeon Barrow is the fireman on the left and the other fireman was named Matter (or Mahar). The engine house still stands at the corner of Walnut and Edwards. *Courtesy Wilbur Barrow*

TOP: Springfield firemen in front of Engine House No. 2 on the north side of Jefferson Street between Third and Fourth streets, circa 1890. *Courtesy Sangamon Valley Collection, Lincoln Library*

ABOVE: Troops leaving Camp Lincoln, circa 1902. *Courtesy Dave Miller*

TOP: Mail delivery method in the early 1900s. Charles Orville Foster was the postman for the Statehouse building at the time this photo was taken. *Courtesy R. L. and Carolyn Moore*

TOP LEFT: Old Illinois State Capitol, circa 1895. Likely was used as Sangamon County building. *Courtesy Sangamon Valley Collection, Lincoln Library*

BOTTOM LEFT: Interior of the Illinois House chamber of the Illinois State Capitol Building, circa 1900. *Courtesy Sangamon Valley Collection, Lincoln Library*

ABOVE: The south side of the Illinois State Capitol, facing what was then Charles Street. Stones purchased for the south portico were stored on the grounds. Because the city would not turn over Charles Street to the state, the portico was never built. Notice the wooden plank used to slide packages down to the waiting carriage. The city finally turned Charles Street over to the state in 1917. *Courtesy Jack Klintworth*

ABOVE: Metcalf & Co. Ambulance provided emergency care for patrons of the Illinois State Fair, 1910.
Courtesy Wilson Park

ABOVE: Springfield Hospital and Training School nurses. The hospital, founded in April 1897, was at Fifth Street and North Grand Avenue. *Courtesy Sangamon Valley Collection, Lincoln Library*

LEFT: The Illinois National Guard at the entrance to Camp Lincoln, circa 1907. *Courtesy Bobby Dorsey*

OPPOSITE: Springfield Firehouse No. 6, circa 1910. The second person from the left is identified as Patrick Richard Hayes.
Courtesy Richard Hayes Lefferts

ABOVE: A large crowd gathers to hear Gov. Louis L. Emmerson and President Herbert Hoover speak in Springfield, circa 1930.
Courtesy Springfield YMCA

RIGHT: Construction of a tunnel under the track at the Illinois State Fairgrounds, 1920s. *Courtesy Mary Sneed*

ABOVE: Rev. Dr. John T. Thomas leads a procession from First Presbyterian Church, followed by city detectives as pallbearers, for their fallen friend and associate Porter Williams, September 1932. *Courtesy Sangamon Valley Collection, Lincoln Library*

BELOW: President Franklin D. Roosevelt, Democratic nominee for president (second term) visits Springfield for drought conference, September 4, 1936. *Courtesy Sangamon Valley Collection, Lincoln Library*

ABOVE: Workmen place pieces of pre-cast concrete on the Illinois Statehouse dome in 1932 when a new roof was installed on the dome. *Courtesy Flo Boner*

RIGHT: View of the curving stairway around the wall supporting the dome and the inner structural framework, 1932. *Courtesy Jack Klintworth*

Lincoln

Abraham Lincoln was 30 years old when Louis Daguerre took the first photograph of a person. But less than 20 years later, Lincoln became the first presidential candidate to make extensive use of the new art in his election campaign, and by the time he died, Lincoln was considered the most photographed person of his day.

That photographic tradition carried over after his death to Lincoln sites in Springfield, beginning with the arrival of the Lincoln funeral train at the Chicago and Alton Depot on May 3, 1865 (p. 97). Local photographers, professional and amateur, regularly recorded famous, and not-so-famous, visitors to Lincoln's home and tomb and chronicled the series of rebuilding and repair projects at the tomb in its early years.

When President Herbert Hoover rededicated the tomb after another rehabilitation in 1931 (p. 100), he accurately summed up the reasons that places associated with Lincoln continued to hold their fascination for visitors:

No man gazes upon the tomb of Lincoln without reflection upon his transcendent qualities of patience, fortitude, and steadfastness. The very greatness which history and popular imagination have stamped upon him sometimes obscures somewhat the real man back of the symbol which he has become. It is not amiss to reflect that he was a man before becoming a symbol. To appreciate the real meaning of his life, we need to contemplate him as the product of the people themselves, as the farm boy, the fence builder, the soldier, the country lawyer, the political candidate, the legislator, and the President, as well as the symbol of union and of human rights.

Time sifts out the essentials of men's character and deeds, and in Lincoln's character there stands out his patience, his indomitable will, his sense of humanity of a breadth which comes to but few men. Of his deeds those things which remain in the memory of every schoolchild in America are the preservation of the Union, the emancipation of the slaves, the infusion of the new conception of popular government. Those are the transcendent services for which he is enshrined by his countrymen. In these accomplishments Lincoln not alone saved the Union, emancipated a race, and restored the Government to the people, but made the United States a power so potent in the world as to turn the tide of human affairs.

LEFT: A horse-drawn wagon gives locals a ride to President Abraham Lincoln's homestead at Eighth and Jackson streets, circa 1901. Roy Ide is the only one identified in the back seat.
Courtesy Sangamon Valley Collection, Lincoln Library

ABOVE: Mourners gather in front of the Lincoln home, which was draped for the funeral in 1865. *The State Journal-Register archives*

RIGHT: This was one of a series of four portraits taken in Springfield, June 3, 1860, by Alexander Hesler of Chicago. Hesler was asked to take some campaign pictures of the candidate. Lincoln couldn't make it to Chicago but agreed to get "dressed up" for the sitting if Hesler would come to Springfield. He did and the photos were taken near a large window in what is now the Old State Capitol. *The State Journal-Register archives*

BELOW: Globe Tavern at the time of Lincoln's funeral, 1865. *Courtesy Sangamon Valley Collection, Lincoln Library*

ABOVE: Illinois State Arsenal draped for Lincoln's funeral, April 1865. The arsenal construction began in 1855 but was not completed until after the Civil War. *Courtesy Sangamon Valley Collection, Lincoln Library*

ABOVE: Old No. 57, the Chicago and Alton Railroad engine that pulled President Lincoln's train at the Springfield Depot, April 1865. The building behind the train is the Metropolitan Mill between Washington and Jefferson streets. *Courtesy Sangamon Valley Collection, Lincoln Library*

LEFT: Demolition of what is believed to be Globe Tavern, October 1893.
Courtesy Sangamon Valley Collection, Lincoln Library

ABOVE: Rededication of the Lincoln Tomb, 1901. In 1901, the Lincoln Tomb, in Oak Ridge Cemetery, was considered unsafe and was taken down and rebuilt. *Courtesy Sangamon Valley Collection, Lincoln Library*

TOP RIGHT: Rebuilding Lincoln's tomb.
Courtesy Sangamon Valley Collection, Lincoln Library

BOTTOM RIGHT: Construction work continues on the rebuild of the Lincoln Tomb in Springfield, circa 1899. The obelisk was increased by 15 feet, and the steel and concrete vault containing Lincoln's remains were buried beneath the floor of the burial chamber.
Courtesy Sangamon Valley Collection, Lincoln Library

ABOVE: Reconstruction of Lincoln's tomb.
Courtesy Sangamon Valley Collection, Lincoln Library

TOP LEFT: A postcard commemorating the centennial of Abraham Lincoln's birth. *Courtesy Virginia Scott*

FAR LEFT: A second remodeling of Lincoln's tomb in 1930.
Courtesy Sangamon Valley Collection, Lincoln Library

LEFT: Charles Lindbergh visits Oak Ridge Cemetery and Lincoln's tomb. *Courtesy Julie Baliva*

ABOVE: Dignitaries and Gov. Louis L. Emmerson greeted Gov. Franklin D. Roosevelt, Democratic candidate for president at Lincoln's tomb, October 21, 1932. Among others in the group were Edward J. Hughes, Federal Judge Louis Fitzhenry, Walter Nesbit, Bruce Campbell, James Roosevelt (son of the governor), Judge Henry Horner and Edward J. Barrett. The order of those identified is unknown.
Courtesy Sangamon Valley Collection, Lincoln Library

LEFT: Duke Ellington at Lincoln's tomb, Nov. 5, 1939. *The State Journal-Register archives*

OPPOSITE: After a two-year reconstruction of the tomb's interior, President Herbert Hoover speaks at the rededication ceremony, June 17, 1931. *The State Journal-Register archives*

Community

Births, confirmations, birthdays, weddings, club meetings, reunions and funerals — in yesteryear as well as today, those were occasions for photographs. There were some differences, of course. A family portrait might well include the horse and rig. A backyard potato patch was a source of pride. And whatever happened to kids riding in goat carts?

Some photo subjects remained as stiff as their celluloid collars. The Capital City Cycling Club was known in the 1880s and '90s as a fun-filled group. ("Quartets, with the help of Ed Coe's bass voice, rendered selections as they pedaled, such as 'Wait Till the Sun Shines Nellie,'" reported a 1931 newspaper article. " 'Twas a gay time. And everybody was well supplied with gum.") But the stalwart cyclists none-theless stared glumly ahead when confronted by a photographer (p.113).

As photography became more advanced, cameras more widespread and their users more proficient, however, photos of even commonplace events took on elements of whimsy, and sometimes art. A generously moustached professional photographer had fun with a triple exposure in the 1890s (p. 109). An obviously posed photo of a dozen boys enjoying giant slices of watermelon in 1905 (p. 114) jumps out of the frame because one boy broke ranks to laugh at his friends. And members of a rough-and-ready contract threshing crew joked with each other while being photographed at the end of a long, hot day in 1917 (p. 122).

LEFT: Mrs. Joseph D. Myers' residence at 615 South Seventh Street, late 1800s. The family owned a carriage company called Myers & Van Duyn. *Courtesy Sangamon Valley Collection, Lincoln Library*

RIGHT: This was probably the first orchestra of serious pretensions in Springfield, circa 1866. It was organized shortly after the Civil War and the players were wearing Union officers' uniforms, purchased for their public appearances. Guido Goldschmidt, at extreme left, was the leader of the group, which played concerts, theatrical performances and society balls. Members pictured are Guido Goldschmidt, Jacob Alyea, Leon Hopkins, John Wienold, Charles Graeser, Franz Xavier Merkle and Henry Eifert. *Courtesy Sangamon Valley Collection, Lincoln Library*

OPPOSITE: The home of John Frederick (Fritz) and Pauline Girard Maisenbacher at 705 North Grand Avenue East, circa 1885. Fritz was born in Springfield in 1858, a son of Mathias and Margarette (Myers) Maisenbacher, natives of Wurtenber, Germany, who came to Springfield in 1848. Fritz is the man with his hand on the chair. His wife is seated with a small child standing near. The man near the horse is Fritz's brother William and to his left is their mother, Margarette. The little girl in front of the fence is Anna Marie Maisenbacher Mueller, grandmother of Nancy M. Hahn. *Courtesy Nancy M. Hahn*

BELOW: Old Roll home at the southwest corner of Second and Cook streets, circa 1876. It was the residence of the late John E. Roll and was in possession of his family for a number of decades. It was built in 1860 and reflected the architectural style of the period. This home was later occupied by Attorney General Edward Akin and then occupied by Logan Coleman. Mr. Coleman sold the house to John S. Schnepp in 1925 and the house was razed to make room for an apartment building. *Courtesy Sangamon Valley Collection, Lincoln Library*

BELOW: The cornerstone for the construction of the third building of the Second Presbyterian Church is laid with the second building in the background at the northwest corner of Fourth and Monroe streets, April 29, 1869. The church has been known as Westminster Presbyterian since 1919. *Courtesy Westminster Presbyterian*

ABOVE: Trinity Lutheran Church under construction, 1889. The church is at Second and Monroe streets. *Courtesy Deborah L. Owens Trinity Lutheran Church Archives*

TOP RIGHT: Interior of the third building of the Second Presbyterian Church, circa 1885. The church has been known as Westminster Presbyterian since 1919. *Courtesy Westminster Presbyterian*

BOTTOM RIGHT: Orchestra La' Allegro, organized by William D. Chenery for the Sunday school of the Second Presbyterian Church, circa 1889. From left, front row are Frank Leeder and Charles Harrison. Middle row are Alfred Killius, Burke Vancil, Charles Maurer, Herman Fifer, Henry Goldsmith, Alfred Lambert, Henry Loeb, and Thomas Owens. Back row are Lee Hickox, visitor, Fred Killius, Robert Reiner, Harris Hickox, Henry Leeder, Harry Blodgett, William D. Chenery, Sylvester Whipple, Frank Harrison, director Eben Hopkins, and August Kessberger. *Courtesy Sangamon Valley Collection, Lincoln Library*

ABOVE: Wedding photo of Mr. and Mrs. George Mull, on left, late 1800s. Also in the photo are Anna Marie King and Logan Chapman. *Courtesy Lesa King Bergeron*

TOP LEFT: The Eben Willey family, circa 1890. From left, seated, Emily Moulton Willey Buscher, Eben Glover Willey, Nellie Hopkins Willey, and Cora Stillwell Willey John. Standing, Richard Oglesby Willey, Caleb Hopkins Willey, John Freeman Willey, Charles Leon Willey, and George Dennis Barker Hopkins Willey. Eben and Nellie had 14 children. The dog in the picture is named Brock. *Courtesy Bernice Rogers*

BOTTOM LEFT: Ss. Peter and Paul Catholic Church picnic at Carpenter Park, 1890. Clara Neef Goulet is the little girl on the right in the first row. Mary Davis is standing behind Clara Neef Goulet. Note the men seated and women standing, ready to serve. *Courtesy Bernard Goulet*

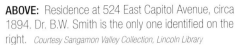

ABOVE: Residence at 524 East Capitol Avenue, circa 1894. Dr. B.W. Smith is the only one identified on the right. *Courtesy Sangamon Valley Collection, Lincoln Library*

TOP RIGHT: Professor Blood's Ladies Orchestra, circa 1890. Members, known as "Professor Blood's Ladies," were from Ss. Peter and Paul Catholic Church. Seated from left are Miss Maggie Maisenbacher, Miss Lucy Franz, Professor Fred Blood, Miss Nan Bernard and Miss Marie Bernard. Standing, Miss Louis Peter, Miss Minnie Nuess and Miss Anna Nuess. *Courtesy Sangamon Valley Collection, Lincoln Library*

BOTTOM RIGHT: GAR officers of Stephenson Post 30, circa 1891. *Courtesy Jim Springer*

ABOVE: Burke Vancil, local photographer, as seen in a trick shot with three different poses, 1890s. *Courtesy Sangamon Valley Collection, Lincoln Library*

TOP LEFT: Henry and Emilie (Garlo) Schroll family at their home, 1895. The area is now under Lake Springfield, just north of Cotton Hill Park. *Courtesy Barb Schroll*

TOP MIDDLE: The Cone Farm, west of Springfield, March 17, 1895. This is now the location of the Koke Mill Subdivision, 1309 Wood Mill Drive. Standing in front is Willie Cone. In back, from left, Charley Cone, Jane Dryer Cone, Mamie Hunt and Will Cone. *Courtesy Jim Springer*

BOTTOM LEFT: Coffee "Klotch" members, late 1800s. This group of women were part of a coffee club in Springfield. Members, from left are Mrs. Krueger, Emma Wieties, Ida Wieties, Mrs. Ramey, unidentified, unidentified, Mrs. Hendricks, Lizzie Butcher and Mrs. Goodwin. *Courtesy Debbie Barrow*

ABOVE: Members of the Old Lincoln Lodge No. 5 of the Independent Order of Mutual Aid, circa 1895. *Courtesy Sangamon Valley Collection, Lincoln Library*

RIGHT: Lillian Eielson and her son, Harry, 1898. *Courtesy Nancy Bryant*

FAR RIGHT: Mrs. Martin J. (Nettie) Baum with her three eldest children, circa 1898. Clockwise from top, Alice Baum who married J. Clarence Lukeman, who started Lukeman Bros. Clothiers in Jacksonville; Elmer Baum, third generation owner of the Baum Monument and Stone Company; and Beatrice Baum who married Carl Fisherkeller and started the B & F Toggery Clothiers in Springfield. *Courtesy Berning Family*

ABOVE: Jeremiah "Jedd" King's residence at 305 South Douglas Avenue, circa 1900. It was his first house after leaving the farm.
Courtesy Mary Elmore and Lesa King Bergeron

TOP LEFT: A group poses on the porch of a house located at 707 North 14th Street, circa 1900. The house was located next door to A.J. Zanders Meat Market. The young man in the center is identified as Anton J. Zanders who would later own the grocery store.
Courtesy Marilyn Stalets

BOTTOM LEFT: National Masonic convention, Sangamon County delegation. *Courtesy Sangamon Valley Collection, Lincoln Library*

BELOW: United Brethren Church Sunday school class, circa 1901.
Courtesy Frances (Hendricks) Loew

ABOVE: Salisbury Christian Church members, 1901. *Courtesy Karla Krueger*

OPPOSITE: One of the most famous organizations ever to ride the streets of Springfield, the Capital City Cycling Club. The photograph, taken in 1901, shows a large part of the club on an outing to the Young Brothers farm, then located east of the city. Many a well-known resident spent hour after hour bicycling on both short and overnight jaunts with fellow members of the club. *Courtesy Sangamon Valley Collection, Lincoln Library*

ABOVE: Mary Catherine Edmands, 1904. *Courtesy Nancy Chapin*

RIGHT: Benjamin Ferguson residence at 815 North Fifth Street, decorated for President Theodore Roosevelt's visit, June 4, 1903. Mr. Ferguson died on June 2, 1903, two days before the president's visit. Mrs. Ferguson passed away March 7, 1921. The home was built by Springfield architect Samuel A. Bullard in 1880. *Courtesy Sangamon Valley Collection, Lincoln Library*

ABOVE: George Lee residence on Clear Lake Avenue, 1906. At the time of the photo, Pleasant Hill School across the street was being built and classes were held in the Lees' home. *Courtesy Sangamon Valley Collection, Lincoln Library*

TOP LEFT: Laying of the cornerstone of the fourth and present building of the Second Presbyterian Church at the corner of Walnut and Edwards streets, September 17, 1906. The church has been known as Westminster Presbyterian since 1919. *Courtesy Westminster Presbyterian*

TOP MIDDLE: Hazel Bates (Wilson) high school graduation photo, 1907. She was the mother of recently deceased Col. John Wilson, whom one of Springfield's post offices may be named after. *Courtesy Dr. Victoria Nichols Johnson*

BOTTOM LEFT: James C. Conkling residence at 801 South Sixth Street, circa 1907. This home also was used as the Wabash, St. Louis & Pacific Railroad Co. Hospital. *Courtesy Sangamon Valley Collection, Lincoln Library*

OPPOSITE: George Edward Day Jr.'s birthday party, circa 1905. *Courtesy Sangamon Valley Collection, Lincoln Library*

ABOVE: Family members in front of Robert Kerneghen cottage, circa 1909. *Courtesy Sangamon Valley Collection, Lincoln Library*

TOP LEFT: A meeting of the Springfield Dental Society at Lincoln Inn, circa 1909. This photo was taken soon after the pavilion at Lincoln Park had been opened to the public. Identified are Ezra F. Hazell, Ben M. Smith, Owen Frazee, Thomas P. Donelan, Robert Booth, James B. Watts, Ben L. Kirby, E. Lambert, Edwin Kartack, Frederick Bowman, Otto H. Seifert, Arthur J. Williams, George H. Henderson, John J. Donelan, William H. Watts, Alfred Lambert, Albert E. Converse, and L. J. Goodson. The order of those identified is unknown. *Courtesy Sangamon Valley Collection, Lincoln Library*

OPPOSITE: Wedding of Rose Stein and Harry Schnepp in 1910. Included in the photo are Susie Kienzler, Rose Stein, bride; Helma Stein, sister of bride; Theresa Wochner, Roy Schnepp, brother of groom; and Harry Schnepp, groom. The order of those identified is unknown. *Courtesy Donna Griffin*

BELOW: St. Mary's Grade School graduation class, 1908. Sister Columbia Otis is in the center. The school was on the northeast corner of Seventh and Monroe streets. Front row, from left are Joe Murphy, Anna Kerwin, Sister Columbia, Tommy Phillips, and Marie Stevens. Second row, Katie Keeley, J.R. Fitzpatrick, Marie Raylotts, Mary Giblin, James Donelan, and Helen Fitzpatrick. Back row, Marie Mulcahy, Tommy Walsh, Ann Hogan, Tom Cullen, Helen Gaffigan, William "Zip" Ryan, unidentified, and Otto Kieble. *Courtesy Sangamon Valley Collection, Lincoln Library*

ABOVE: A Springfield street crowded with what is thought to be movers moving furnishings and other effects to the new Masonic Temple, which was completed and dedicated in December 1909. *Courtesy F. Richard Carlson, Sec/Rec Springfield York Rite Bodies*

ABOVE: Thomas "Tom" Maurice (pronounced "Morris") Lawrence Sr., Nettie (Barnstable) Lawrence and Thomas Maurice Lawrence Jr. on the porch of their home at 1512 Holmes Avenue, circa 1910. The home was originally at 1416 Holmes Avenue. Tom was head of the local Armour meat-packing plant until shortly after Nettie died in 1911. He quit his job and rented out his house, bought half ownership in the Princess (later the Lincoln) Theatre, and finally left town. His son Thomas moved in with another family and later went away to college. Tom Jr. became an insurance and bond salesman and lived at the Elks Club. He married after his father's death in 1946 when he was nearly 50 years old. Tom Jr. passed away in 1991. *Courtesy Sangamon Valley Collection, Lincoln Library*

ABOVE: Four generations of the Schnepp family, circa 1911. Clockwise from the top, Harry Schnepp, Jacob Schnepp, Loretta Schnepp (baby) and great-grandfather Fletcher Haines. *Courtesy Donna Griffin*

LEFT: Katie and Patrick Hayes in the potato patch behind their home at 116 South Glenwood Avenue, circa 1910. *Courtesy Richard Hayes Lefferts*

ABOVE: Trinity Lutheran School pupils, circa 1912. The man below one of the windows on the far right is teacher F.C. Diesing. *Courtesy Clara Sotak*

LEFT: Groundbreaking ceremony for the First Christian Church, June 4, 1911. Mrs. Caroline Kane is holding the shovel and her son, Charles P. Kane, is standing next to her on the left. This was the former site of the Iles home. *Courtesy Sangamon Valley Collection, Lincoln Library*

BELOW: James Alfred Greer, born in January 1900, delivering the State Journal or Register in 1910. His daughter, sons, granddaughter, grandson and great-granddaughters live in Springfield. *Courtesy Helen Greer Cox*

ABOVE: Wedding photo of William and Margaret Trotter, 1913. William was the grandson of George Trotter, an early settler in Springfield, moving to the area in 1835 with his wife Mary Anna and daughter Agnes Dickson Trotter. George was friends and business associates with Pascal Enos and Elijah Iles. Agnes Trotter married Zimri Enos, son of Pascal Enos. Margaret Trotter was the daughter of William Frederick and Margaretha Anna Bickes. William was the caretaker of Oak Ridge Cemetery when Abraham Lincoln's body was stolen. Five of their six children were born in the caretaker's house that used to be inside the cemetery. *Courtesy Michael Leckrone*

RIGHT: Bertha Mae Corven Wilson, 1914. *Courtesy Sandra Colborn*

ABOVE: Members of the John L. Taylor Ensemble, circa 1915. The man at left is John Starr Stewart. John was the music critic for the State Journal. *Courtesy Constance Locher Bussard*

RIGHT: Antoinette Meyer in her tennis outfit, 1912. *Courtesy Dorothy Ewing*

OPPOSITE: Printers' Drum and Bugle Corp getting ready for the Labor Day Parade in 1914. Included in the photo are Roy Thornberg, unidentified, George Lischer, Mr. Campbell, William Bruening, Mr. Buedel, Daniel Boehnert, Arthur Bea, Mace Shumate, Tony Davis, L.A. Freeman, Alex Farnsworth, Mr. Barch, Leslie Knight, Clinton C. Dye. The order of those identified is unknown. *Courtesy Sangamon Valley Collection, Lincoln Library*

ABOVE: Mary Milligan playing nurse with her uncle, Carl Becker, 1917. *Courtesy Clarissa Milligan Cullen*

TOP LEFT: Confirmation photo of Dora and Louie Renker, circa 1917. *Courtesy Shirley M. Springer*

BOTTOM LEFT: Walter Smith in his World War I uniform, circa 1917. *Courtesy Elizabeth Hamrick*

FAR LEFT: Ostermeier threshing rig operated by brothers William, Henry and Frederick Ostermeier, their 12 sons and hired men. They would travel from farm to farm and harvest for other farmers as well as their own farms. Photo taken at Maple Hill Farm, rural Springfield, 1917. *Courtesy Susan Ostermeier Tesar*

ABOVE: George Webster residence at the northeast corner of the Illinois State Fairgrounds, 2925 Peoria Road, 1918. Family members, from left are George (father), Kay, Elizabeth, John (children), Catherine (mother) and Hannah, daughter. George, Catherine and Hannah immigrated from England to Springfield in 1905. The other children were born in Springfield. George was a mining union official.
Courtesy Susan Ostermeier Tesar

LEFT: Twins George and Eloise Price have their picture taken with their younger sister June on a goat cart in their front yard on Milton Avenue, 1920.
Courtesy Larry and Kay Price

ABOVE: Madeline and James Whiteside, circa 1920.
Courtesy Rose Lambert

LEFT: Pete and Clarissa Milligan in a goat cart at Holmes Avenue, 1924. In the 1920s, a traveling photographer would come through the neighborhood and take pictures of children in his goat cart.
Courtesy Clarissa Milligan Cullen

BELOW: Funeral procession for Anna Mazrim, February 14, 1919. Anna fell victim to the flu epidemic. *Courtesy James R. McIntyre*

ABOVE: Springfield Stockyards, circa 1920. *Courtesy Lucille Martinek*

TOP LEFT: Roche's Society Orchestra, a very popular group during the 1920s. They played at many dances throughout the Springfield area. In 1924, they presented a special concert on radio station KSD in St. Louis and received many fine comments. From left are Dewey Blaine, drums; Gene Matthews, banjo; Jimmy Roche, piano; Ernest Smith, saxophone and Ernest McAvin, trumpet. *Courtesy Marsha Jones*

BOTTOM LEFT: Caroline Ostermeier pins a boutonniere on her son, Robert C. Ostermeier, prior to Springfield High School's senior play, 1921. *Courtesy Eden Lindberg*

BELOW: In 1924, a meeting was called by Mrs. Lewis Miner at her home to establish a group devoted to ceramics. When the 12 women met at her home on May 21, 1924, little did they realize that they were to be the nucleus of an organization that was someday to be one of the leading cultural groups, a group that not only gives its members an opportunity for full expression of their artistic talents, but also brings art to women. Later the club would be known as the Springfield Ceramics and Crafts Club. In this photo, members were celebrating the 15th anniversary of the founding of the club, May 1939. Officers elected at the first meeting were: Mrs. Lewis Miner, president; Miss Mary Newell, vice-president; Mrs. Howard Layman, treasurer; and Mrs. Edward (Knox) Madden, secretary. *Courtesy Susanne Wall*

ABOVE: Children and their ponies on the Woodruff Farm, 1925. The children are Elmer Boehme, Ray Woodruff, Joseph Murch and Mary Woodruff (O'Brian). *Courtesy Dorothy Ross*

TOP LEFT: Dr. H.F. Kovski of Kovski and Kovski Chiropractic poses in front of the Illinois State Capitol in 1926.
Courtesy Kory M. Kovski and Lindsay Kovski

TOP RIGHT: Girl Scouts standing on Jackson Street alongside Christ Episcopal Church, circa 1925. *Courtesy Sangamon Valley Collection, Lincoln Library*

RIGHT: Groundbreaking ceremony for the new structure for Laurel Methodist Church on the northeast corner of Walnut Street and South Grand Avenue in 1924. *Courtesy Sangamon Valley Collection, Lincoln Library*

TOP LEFT: Werner and O'Brian children, circa 1926. First child on left is Bill Werner then Noreen O'Brian; third boy is Charles Werner. The rest of the children are O'Brians. *Courtesy Carol Werner*

BOTTOM LEFT: These men fought in Grant's regiment in the Civil War. Included in the group is Albert Armstrong, who ran away from home at age 16 to fight in the Civil War. These men met by this tree (Grant's Tree) to commemorate being together in Grant's encampment. Unfortunately, the tree was destroyed by lightning. A farmer used the wood from the tree to make mementoes for his family. There is now a memorial at the site of the tree. *Courtesy Pat Kienzler*

FAR LEFT: George and Margaret White in hot air balloon, "Flying High" in Krug Park, 1920s. *Courtesy Jerry White*

ABOVE: Sunday school of the Third Presbyterian Church, June 5, 1927. There were 1,433 in attendance. *Courtesy Donald L. Harvey*

RIGHT: Members of Springfield Woman's Club proudly display a newspaper article written about their organization, 1920s. *Courtesy Sangamon Valley Collection, Lincoln Library*

OPPOSITE LEFT: Bishop Griffin with servers, Easter 1926 or 1927. Front row, from left are Edward Unger and Raymond Cicci. Second row, Charles McCue, James Furlong, John Mayol, Paul Graham, William Reedy, Joseph Phillips, Edward Gaffigan, George Suddes, Edward Lucasey, Charles Ross, and Thomas Higgins. Third row, Imard Mayfield, Reynolds Mayol, Joseph Corrigan, John Murphy, Vincent Vespa, Joseph Daughton, Peter McCue, Frank LaBarbara, William McGrath, Francis Lucasey, John Gaffigan, and Tony Cersoli. Fourth row, Harry Bixler, Gerald Gilkerson, Francis Corrigan, Charles Whalen, John Corrigan, William McGough, Alph Corrigan, William Furlong, James Daughton, Carrol Wilderson, and Stuart McCulley. Fifth row, Nicholas Reilly, Sam Bonansinga, Joseph Joy, Edward McCue, Robert Ambrose, Thomas Suddes, Thomas Gilmore, Lawrence Melton, and Albert Hagele. Sixth row, John Reedy, John Donovan, Alvin Layton, Francis Flannigan, Claude Goldsberry, Thomas White, William Levis, Neil McGinnis, Patrick Kelly, and Hugh Gallagher. Seventh row, Richard White, Roy Gilkerson, Thomas Hogan, James Suddes, Walter Gaffigan, Paul Beaghan, Thomas DeMarco, Michael Connors, and Thomas Connors. Eighth row, George Mayfield, Joseph Hogan, Frank Bonansinga, Bishop James A. Griffin, John Ryan, Franci McGuire, Joseph Bonansinga, and John Higgins. *Courtesy Goulet Melton Family*

OPPOSITE TOP RIGHT: Robert Dickerman, James Dickerman and Mrs. Ruth Dickerman all dressed up for the first Beaux Arts of Springfield Art Association costume party in 1929. *Courtesy Barbara Dickerman*

OPPOSITE BOTTOM RIGHT: From left, Vesta Meek (Nichols), Russell Meek and Dorothy Meek (Brooks), circa 1928. *Courtesy Dr. Victoria Nichols Johnson*

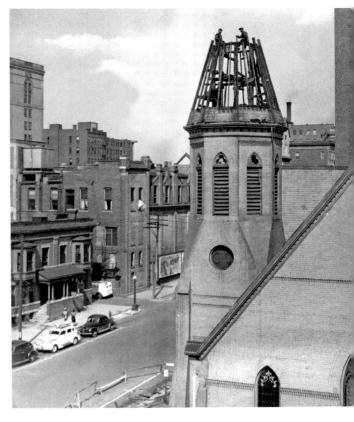

ABOVE: Clara (Dodd) Sotak in goat cart in front of her home at 1609 South 11th Street, 1930. *Courtesy Clara Sotak*

RIGHT: Georgia Artis on the family farm in Buffalo Hart, 1929. She passed away when she was 98 years old. *Courtesy Joyce L. Beard*

ABOVE: Workers remove the steeple of Central Baptist Church at Fourth Street and Capitol Avenue in 1930 after it was declared unstable. *Courtesy Central Baptist Archives*

TOP MIDDLE RIGHT: Joe Hogan, local boxer at YMCA, 1930. At the Middle-States AAU matches in Gary, Ind., Hogan beat the famous Tony Zale. Tony Zale later became middle champion of the world. *Courtesy Robert J. Hogan*

LEFT: Handmade concrete lion, 1929. The lion still stands in Springfield outside Lanphier High School at the 11th Street entrance. *Courtesy Edward Schuler*

OPPOSITE: Third Presbyterian Church Christian Endeavor group, 1929. Rev. Hildebrandt and wife are in the first row, fourth and fifth seat. Herb Bergman is in the first row, sixth seat. *Courtesy Debbie Barrow*

ABOVE: Boy Scout Troop No. 1 was the first troop in Springfield. Here, they point to the face and toes of their leader, John William Brown. He was covered with sand near the Sangamon River. The Boy Scouts met at Wesley United Methodist Church. *Courtesy Marilyn Lane*

TOP RIGHT: West Side Christian Church members, 1931. Rev. Laverne Taylor was the pastor at the time of this photograph. *Courtesy Sangamon Valley Collection, Lincoln Library*

BOTTOM RIGHT: Ritcher family, from left, Norman T. Richter, Max F. Richter, Joseph E. Richter and Isabella (Temple) Richter. *Courtesy Nancy (Richter) Lashbrook, David Richter and Janet Richter*

OPPOSITE LEFT: Bertha M. (Corven) Wilson competed for Sangamon County Queen at the Fourth of July pageant in 1932. Bertha was chosen as queen but gave the title to the runner-up. George, her soon-to-be husband, didn't want the publicity. *Courtesy Sandra Colborn*

OPPOSITE TOP RIGHT: Butch Schafer of Schafer & Sons Hatchery holds a chicken in front of a sign announcing winnings of the hatchery, 1932. *Courtesy Sharon Schafer Kording*

OPPOSITE BOTTOM RIGHT: Nearly 200 unemployed men welcome Firestone's plan to "Place Dollars in Their Pockets." They sold coupon books that netted them cash for Firestone Service stores at 415 South Sixth Street in May 1932. *Courtesy Sangamon Valley Collection, Lincoln Library*

Joe Schafer & Sons
HATCHERY
The Hatchery of Quality & Service
SPRINGFIELD, ILL.

1931 · Winnings · 1932
6 Firsts   9 Firsts
3 Seconds   5 Seconds
5 Thirds   4 Thirds

Baby Chicks For Sale Now.

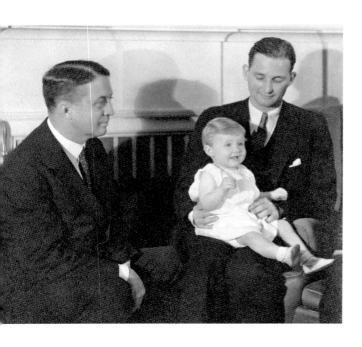

ABOVE: Robert C. Lanphier, left, with his son Robert C. Lanphier Jr., right, who is holding his son, Robert C. Lanphier III. *Courtesy Nancy Chapin*

TOP RIGHT: A family gathering after the funeral of Thomas Artis, who was more than 100 years old. The Artis twins, Corrine and Lorrine are in the back row. Lorrine is on the far left, then her father, Orville and the other twin, Corrine. Vera Artis Murrell is in the middle row, third from left. Others also in the photo are, Henry Artis, D'Arcy Artis, Ethel Artis Wheatley, Oney Artis and Minnie Artis. *Courtesy Joyce L. Beard*

BOTTOM RIGHT: Second Constitutional Convention of the Illinois Women's Auxiliary, Progressive Miners of America members, 1933. *Courtesy Catherine Mans*

OPPOSITE TOP LEFT: Wersella and Norbert Lemons at 2004 South Collage Street, at the Fox residence, 1934. *Courtesy Sharon McMullen*

OPPOSITE TOP RIGHT: Driver, Mike Connolly, president of the Ducs Club, enjoys a sunny day with friends, 1934. The photo was taken at 1144 North Eighth Street. *Courtesy Dan Connolly*

ABOVE: Catholic Boy Choristers, 1930s. Rev. George Windsor was the director. *Courtesy Sangamon Valley Collection, Lincoln Library*

LEFT: Members of Fifth Presbyterian Church at 2139 East Capitol Avenue, 1930s. *Courtesy Sangamon Valley Collection, Lincoln Library*

BELOW: Lioness Club members in front of Dr. Morgan's house, 300 block, South Seventh Street.
Courtesy Sangamon Valley Collection, Lincoln Library

ABOVE: Five- and 6-year-old friends with their jump ropes on the sidewalk in front of 511 Broad Place in 1936. From left, Jean Crump, Helen Sellers, Shirley Fisher and Charlotte Murphy. *Courtesy Helen Brooks*

TOP RIGHT: Family reunion at Washington Park, 1937. Front row are Billy Howard, Howard Green, Jim Green, Ed Waters, Jo Frances Goeke, Mary Lee Goeke, Theresa Jones, Rita Roche, Mary Alice Roche, Betty Waters, Mary Waters, Jim Waters, and Bernie Waters. Middle row, Tom Howard, Katie Howard with JoAnn Howard, Mary Waters with Julie Waters, Eliza Howard with Mary F. Howard, Stacie Howard, Grace Waters, Mary Jones, Arama Roche, Anna Green, Julia Waters, Geraldine Waters, and Joan Waters. Back row, Francis Howard, Jim Waters, Leo Howard, Ed Roche, Ann Howard, Alice Waters, Georgia Howard, Vincent Howard, Les Jones, John Booker, Irma Booker, Les Green, Mike Waters, and Maurice Green. *Courtesy Jo Ann Davis*

BOTTOM RIGHT: Springfield Orchestra members in the 1930s. *Courtesy Sangamon Valley Collection, Lincoln Library*

ABOVE: Birthday party for Archie Shryver at the Shryver residence, 1937. The birthday boy is on the couch wearing a tie. Identified in the second row are, Sheila Tobin, Eddie Tobin, Ronald Philmon, Jackie Shryver (girl with bow). Also identified is Barb Thiessan (baby on the floor). *Courtesy Debbie Barrow*

TOP LEFT: The "colored" section of the Municipal Band at an old folks outing, 1939. Blacks and whites did not play together until Mayor Nelson Howarth brought them together.
Courtesy Joyce L. Beard

BOTTOM LEFT: St. Paul AME Church leadership meeting, deacons, missionaries and stewards, circa 1939. The meeting was held in the parlor of the parish. *Courtesy Sangamon Valley Collection, Lincoln Library*

FAR LEFT: Birthday party for Patty Ann Lavin, June 28, 1937. In the photo are Marilyn Bernet, Patty Ann Lavin, Frances Lavin and Bobby Bernet. They are in front of the water fountain at Lincoln Park. *Courtesy Mary Frances Lavin*

Tragedy

Fires were frequent and dangerous in early Springfield. Without smoke alarms, sprinkler systems and good equipment, firefighters were at a big disadvantage when facing a fire in a commercial building.

The results could be devastating, as in the 1924 blaze (p. 146) that turned the Myers Brothers Clothing Co. building into a skeleton. (The handsome pre-fire Myers Brothers building is shown on p. 43.) Only two years later, the Logan Hay office building a block away caught fire (p. 147), and eight neighboring businesses suffered damage as well.

Local photographers captured a variety of other calamities over the years — floods, ice storms, derailments, dynamite explosions.

But in terms of lasting damage to Springfield and its reputation, no accidental mishap ever had consequences as disastrous as the race riot of 1908 (pp. 143-44). Seven people were killed, dozens of homes and businesses were destroyed, and the national scandal of a race riot happening in the hometown of Abraham Lincoln resulted in the formation of the National Association for the Advancement of Colored People.

LEFT: Hatcher Service Co. fire, January 19, 1921. The business was at 703-705 East Adams Street. *Courtesy Sangamon Valley Collection, Lincoln Library*

ABOVE: Fire consumed the furniture store of Johnston & Hatcher at Seventh and Adams streets and three adjoining businesses, December 21, 1907. One of the businesses destroyed in the blaze was the Meyer building. Both buildings were again erected.
Courtesy Sangamon Valley Collection, Lincoln Library

TOP RIGHT: A train derailment at Third and Jefferson streets near the downtown business district; only coal gondolas were involved. The train, pulled by a steam engine, was southbound when the cars jumped the track. The pileup resulted in broken power, telephone and telegraph line poles and a portion of the east wall of the Northwestern Hotel was caved in.
Courtesy Sangamon Valley Collection, Lincoln Library

BOTTOM RIGHT: Ruth Martin, left, and Hazel Jones Park walk along the railroad tracks to get a better look at the flooding in Springfield, early 1900s. *Courtesy Karen Alexander*

OPPOSITE: National Guard troops camped on the Statehouse lawn during the race riots in 1908. Gov. Charles Deneen called out 4,000 National Guard troops who arrived on Saturday, August 15.
Courtesy Jack Klintworth

ABOVE: The Second Regiment guarding the Capitol during the race riots of 1908. *Courtesy Randy von Liski*

TOP LEFT: The Capitol grounds during the race riots of 1908. *Courtesy Randy von Liski*

BOTTOM LEFT: Mabel Hallam's alleged rape by a black man in 1908 is what started the race riots in Springfield. *Courtesy Sangamon Valley Collection, Lincoln Library*

BELOW: View of Springfield after the race riot of 1908. Harry Loper's restaurant and an automobile were destroyed. *Courtesy Sangamon Valley Collection, Lincoln Library*

ABOVE: Roland's Clothing Store fire sale, 1915. The store was on the east side of the public square. The fire began on December 7, 1915, as reported in the newspaper. *Courtesy Sangamon Valley Collection, Lincoln Library*

TOP: Fire at Sanford's Furniture, 400 block of East Adams Street, August 1, 1912. *Courtesy Sangamon Valley Collection, Lincoln Library*

LEFT: DeWitt Smith Building fire at Fourth and Monroe streets, March 12, 1918. *Courtesy Sangamon Valley Collection, Lincoln Library*

ABOVE: A view of the tree damage caused by the ice storm of 1924. *Courtesy Nancy Dillon*

BELOW: Van Horn and Link fire, March 18, 1923. The business was at 122 South Sixth Street (east of the public square), and the fire started when two boys used matches as they were trying to rob the store. *Courtesy Sangamon Valley Collection, Lincoln Library*

ABOVE: Myers Brothers Clothing Co. fire at Fifth and Washington streets, March 24, 1924. The cause of the fire was spontaneous combustion of rags and paints left in the basement by painters.
Courtesy Sangamon Valley Collection, Lincoln Library

BELOW: Enos School fire at 524 Elliot Avenue, October 28, 1925. The fire started with faulty wiring in the attic. One teacher was badly burned and overcome with smoke. Nearly 500 children attended this school and were dismissed shortly before the fire was discovered. *Courtesy Sangamon Valley Collection, Lincoln Library*

ABOVE: A fireman was seriously injured, and the engineer and conductor only slightly injured when the Illinois Central engine was hurled down the hill by a dynamite explosion. A pileup of 11 empty freight cars and oil tanks resulted from the explosion in August 1935. *Courtesy Sangamon Valley Collection, Lincoln Library*

BELOW: Logan Hay Office Building fire at Sixth and Washington streets, January 29, 1926. The fire caused widespread damage to several businesses in the public square. Businesses that sustained loss were: Claxpool's drug store, United cigar store, John Buck's barber shop, Maigin Bros. fruit store, Louis Fishman & Son sporting shop, Springfield Photo Finishing, attorney J.W. Shuhan's office, Capitol City Cycling Club and the Hogan Building. *Courtesy Sangamon Valley Collection, Lincoln Library*

Recreation & Celebration

The 1939 Springfield Browns (facing page) were typical of the majority of local minor league baseball teams in the first four decades of the 20th century — they had a middling record, produced no eventual major league stars, and, as a franchise, were short-lived. (For that matter, that track record held true for Springfield teams in most of the decades that followed, too.)

Although records from the 1939 season of the Class B Three-I League are incomplete, the statistics that do exist indicate the Browns, managed by Walter Holke, probably finished fourth among the league's eight teams. Four Brownies — Loy Hanning, Bob Neighbors, George Hausmann and Chuck Stevens — had brief and undistinguished major league careers.

And this edition of the Browns lasted only through the 1942 season, though the team name was revived for a few more years after World War II.

Luckily, Springfieldians had other ways to amuse themselves over the years. You don't see many serious games of marbles anymore (p. 151), but many other long-ago pastimes — parades, family get-togethers, visiting the Illinois State Fair, lazy days at Washington Park or on Lake Springfield — are as popular today as they were decades ago.

LEFT: Springfield Browns, opening day of the Three-I League, 1939. *Courtesy Sangamon Valley Collection, Lincoln Library*

ABOVE: Springfield baseball team, 1890. Identified are, front row, W.C. Garrard, Martin Hazlett, John Picrik and his son Herman Picrik, and Ken Stacy. Back row, Henson Robinson, unknown, Dude Butler, Charles Schuppe, Will Starne. *Courtesy Henson Robinson*

OPPOSITE: Hickox boys playing marbles at South Fourth Street, circa 1900. *Courtesy Sangamon Valley Collection, Lincoln Library*

BELOW: Members of Saltatoria Dancing Club, 1890s. *Courtesy Sangamon Valley Collection, Lincoln Library*

ABOVE: Springfield Yellow Hammer baseball team, circa 1890. *Courtesy Sangamon Valley Collection, Lincoln Library*

TOP: Baseball players who played in the Merchants Bankers Game, circa 1902. *Courtesy Sangamon Valley Collection, Lincoln Library*

ABOVE: Springfield area folks enjoy an afternoon at what is believed to be Washington Park, circa 1912. *Courtesy B. Evelyn Mitchell*

TOP RIGHT: Washington Park, circa 1910. The old boat house is in the distance. *Courtesy Dorothy Ewing*

BOTTOM RIGHT: Showman Barney Oldfield prepares for an Illinois State Fair race in 1905. The car is believed to be the Peerless Mine Special. Known more for his showmanship and bravado than his car racing ability, he raced against airplanes and non-professional drivers. Oldfield was suspended by the American Automobile Association "for life" no less than four times. He won some highly publicized match races, including four of six against Ralph De Palma in 1918, but his Indianapolis career was dismal; fifth place in 1914 and 1916. *Courtesy Sangamon Valley Collection, Lincoln Library*

ABOVE: Paris Cleaners basketball team, 1917-18. Front row from left are O.A. Livingstone, Jenkins, R.S. Livingstone, and J.B. Livingstone. Back row, Taft, Jasper, and A.R. Livingstone.
Courtesy Sangamon Valley Collection, Lincoln Library

BELOW: Automobile racing at the Illinois State Fairgrounds, circa 1925.
Courtesy Sangamon Valley Collection, Lincoln Library

ABOVE: Celebration of the 54th wedding anniversary of Mr. and Mrs. Gerhard Westenberger at the Washington Park Pavilion, February 7, 1914. The two were married in Ss. Peter and Paul Catholic Church February 7, 1860, and from that union had 13 children. For many years, Gerhard Westenberger was in the furniture business in the 400 block of East Adams Street. Identified are, from left, George Thoma, Margaret Westenberger, Mary Westenberger, Herman Helmle, and Frances Bartelme. Second row, Frances Thoma, George Thoma, Mrs. George Thoma, Mrs. Gerhard Westenberger, Gerhard Westenberger, Henry Thoma, Mrs. Henry Thoma, Bert Sutton, Mrs. Bert Sutton, and Robert L Sutton. Third row, George Westenberger, Mrs. George Westenberger, John Westenberger, Mrs. John Westenberger, Herman Maurer with baby Margaret, Mrs. Herman Maurer, and Mrs. Thomas Allen. Fourth row, Mrs. Orlin Barnes with baby Margarethe, Mrs. Laura Thoma McCarthy, Helen Thoma, Mrs. Robert Erdman, Mrs. Ray Simmons, Ray Simmons, Mrs. Cathie Bartelme, and Mrs. Marie Powell. Fifth row, Mrs. Gary Westenberger, Gary Westenberger, P.M. Bartelme, Mrs. Lin McGrath, Newport Powell, and Mrs. Ernst Helmle. Sixth row, Ernst Helmle Jr. and Thomas Allen. *Courtesy Patricia Janssen*

153

ABOVE: Dome Building at the Illinois State Fairgrounds, 1907. The building's huge glass dome, the world's second largest unsupported dome at 222 feet in diameter, had been part of the 1893 Chicago World's Fair. It was purchased for $69,000, taken down in Chicago and reassembled at the state fairgrounds. The building could accommodate 10,000 people. In 1917, about 1,500 soldiers waiting to go to war were temporarily housed in the Dome Building.

On August 17, 1917, the building caught fire. Within 30 minutes after the fire was discovered, the huge glass dome came crashing down. *Courtesy Henry Buckles Family*

RIGHT: Those identified include, standing, H.L. Livingstone, A.R. Livingstone and Roy Cook. Others unidentified, 1925. *Courtesy Sangamon Valley Collection, Lincoln Library*

ABOVE: Columbus Day parade down Capitol Avenue, October 12, 1926. *Courtesy Anna (Vizzini) Danner*

RIGHT: Illinois Bell Telephone Co. baseball team, 1928. Identified are from left, front row, Dave Comeotte, Al Rechner, Joe Hess, Joe Griffin, and Wallace Olshefsky. Back row, John Ushman, Pete Moske, Robert Taylor-Monger, Tom Robinson, and Bob Easley. *Courtesy Patsy Bethard*

BELOW: Panaromic view of the Illinois State Fair, circa 1909. *Courtesy Sangamon Valley Collection, Lincoln Library*

ABOVE: Parade at 611 East Washington Street, 1929. On horse is Nathan Oberman. Front of car is Ben Kirman. Top of car is Harry Perlmutter. Ben Burnstine has his hat in his hand and Harry Burnstine is the gentleman wearing his cap. *Courtesy Bette Kaiserman*

LEFT: William E. Castor Sr. joined the Springfield Motor Boat Club in the spring of 1938 and bought his first boat, pictured here. He is taking it to the gas dock to fill it up for a boat race that day. *Courtesy Bill Castor*

BELOW: President Herbert Hoover rides through town during his welcoming celebration, circa 1930. *Courtesy Springfield YMCA*

BELOW: Thanksgiving Day gathering at the home of Mindie Martin north of Converse Street on Carolina Avenue, circa 1930. Included in the photo are the Beeby, Gibson and Martin families as well as Bobby Stone and Billy Stone. The order of those identified is unknown. *Courtesy Sharen Bucari*

ABOVE: Celebration for William Renken's 75th birthday, May 19, 1939, at 334 North Glenwood Avenue. *Courtesy Shirley M. Springer*

TOP RIGHT: A crowd gathers outside the offices of the State Journal on Sixth Street to follow the baseball game between St. Louis and Philadelphia in 1938. *Courtesy Sangamon Valley Collection, Lincoln Library*

BOTTOM RIGHT: Howard "Zig" Post and his wife Hilda with their sons Donald "007" and Gordon "Diz" Post watching the races at the boat show in 1939. *Courtesy Donald Post*

BELOW: Baum family Easter dinner hosted by Mrs. Martin J. (Nettie) Baum at the Leland Hotel in 1939. Four of her five children are present with their spouses and 15 of the 20 grandchildren. *Courtesy Berning Family*

Index